DIY Programming and Book Displays

DIY Programming and Book Displays

How to Stretch Your Programming without Stretching Your Budget and Staff

Amanda Moss Struckmeyer and Svetha Hetzler

LIBRARIES UNLIMITED

AN IMPRINT OF ABC-CLIO, LLC
Santa Barbara, California • Denver, Colorado • Oxford, England

Copyright 2010 by Amanda Moss Struckmeyer and Svetha Hetzler

Library of Congress Cataloging-in-Publication Data

Struckmeyer, Amanda Moss.
  DIY programming and book displays : how to stretch your programming
  without stretching your budget and staff / Amanda Moss Struckmeyer and
  Svetha Hetzler.
      p. cm.
  Includes bibliographical references and index.
  ISBN 978-1-59884-472-6 (acid-free paper) — ISBN 978-1-59884-473-3 (ebook)
1. Children's libraries—Activity programs—United States.   2. Young adults'
libraries—Activity programs—United States.   3. Library exhibits—United States.
I. Hetzler, Svetha.   II. Title.   III. Title: Do it yourself programming and book displays.
  Z718.3.S77   2010
  027.62'5—dc22   2010024230

ISBN: 978-1-59884-472-6
EISBN: 978-1-59884-473-3

14 13 12 11 10   1 2 3 4 5

This book is also available on the World Wide Web as an eBook.
Visit www.abc-clio.com for details.

Libraries Unlimited
An Imprint of ABC-CLIO, LLC

ABC-CLIO, LLC
130 Cremona Drive, P.O. Box 1911
Santa Barbara, California 93116-1911

This book is printed on acid-free paper ∞

Manufactured in the United States of America

Special thanks to all the DIY participants at the Middleton Public Library.

SH: Thanks to everyone at home for their encouragement— Mark, Monika, Marisa, Jack, and Akhila, and to Bix and his good looks!

AMS: To my project-oriented husband, Karl, and his inspiration, Bob Vila (the original do-it-yourselfer).

Contents

Introduction and Basics

It is no secret that librarians wear many hats. We are customer service providers, catalogers, collection developers, interior decorators, reference and readers' advisory service providers, publicists, Web designers, entertainers, and so much more. Many librarians serve patrons younger than a year old, elementary school-aged children, teens and young adults, adults, parents, seniors, and caregivers. The demands can be daunting, especially when taking into account the constraints of staffing, scheduling, budget, and daily responsibilities.

The Middleton Public Library is a medium-sized suburban library serving an increasingly diverse population. The library's location, near Wisconsin's capital city and a major university, contributes to an increased demand in services and materials. At our library, patrons are always looking for ways to keep themselves active. Sometimes our scheduled programs don't line up with the busy schedules of home, school, and after-school life. We wanted to find a way to make programs accessible to all patrons, regardless of schedules. We also wanted to find a way to expand our program offerings without expanding our staff or our budget. Our solution: DIY (do-it-yourself) programming!

We started out very simply. To celebrate Black History Month, we asked patrons to write down a favorite book by an African American author or illustrator, or a favorite African American character. To get patrons started, we set out a display of books and an accompanying booklist. The preparation was minimal, the program didn't require extra staffing, and the response was very healthy. In just two weeks, over 30 patrons had participated in the program. We offered a tote bag (received as a gift from a vendor) as a prize incentive. From there, our DIY programming evolved into more diverse and engaging activities. The growing popularity of DIY programs has been evidenced in our participation statistics.

In this manual you will find thematic DIY activities that you can use at your library. You can expand these to include non-DIY programming if staffing, schedules, and budget allow. Some of the themes are seasonal but can be easily adjusted to fit your library's needs. For example, our museum DIY activities are suggested for the month of May, National Museum Month; of course, museums might be celebrated any time throughout the year. Each activity includes the purpose, an intended age group, instructions and preparation advice, activity sheets, entry forms, and patterns. You'll also find display ideas and tips for expanding on DIY programs. A thematic booklist, which can be used as a patron handout, is provided at the end of each chapter. These lists, as well as occasional brief booklists that appear with select activities in this book, are good sources of titles to include in displays or in the DIY station book basket.

These activities appeal to library patrons of all ages but especially to youth. Our hope is that this manual will serve youth services librarians in a manner that best suits their professional goals and needs. You may wish to simply reproduce the activity sheets as presented, or you may prefer to use the manual as a springboard to develop and tailor programs to your library patrons' interests. Ultimately, the purpose of *DIY Programming and Book Displays: How to Stretch Your Programming without Stretching Your Budget and Staff* is to present practical, affordable, and easy-to-implement program and display ideas that promote the public library as a center for community, recreation, and lifelong learning.

DIY BASICS

Do-it-yourself (DIY) programming presents a win-win situation for your library patrons: Library visitors have the chance to engage in unique activities, and you are able to provide additional programming without a large investment in time, personnel, or materials. With a few basic materials, a minimal amount of work, and some creativity, you can easily set up and maintain a DIY station that will serve hundreds of patrons each month.

In essence, a DIY station provides an area for library patrons of all ages to find materials and instructions for completing thematic activities at the library. A DIY station can be very simple; the following supplies are recommended:

- A small table
- A brochure holder (a two- or three-tiered model works well) or two or three shallow wire baskets for holding activity sheets
- A raffle box or ballot box
- Acrylic sign holders for instructions
- Pencils and a container to keep them in
- Wall space or a bulletin board nearby for posting materials and displays
- Crayons and a container to keep them in
- A large basket or tub to keep thematic books in (this can be kept on the table or on the floor nearby)

Welcome your library visitors to use the DIY station independently at any time. At our library, we let patrons know about the DIY stations through the newsletter, Web site, and in-library notices. We have a large, colorful "DIY Station" poster hanging above the area.

Choose from the variety of activities available. These might involve coloring, writing, estimating, or creating. A broad selection of activities ensures that most patrons find something that appeals to them. Many visitors will complete more than one DIY activity; some will try all of them!

At the beginning of each month, furnish your DIY station with activities related to a theme. This theme might reflect the season, national holidays, library events, or local

Our basic DIY station, complete with raffle box, book basket, and activities.

happenings. Place instructions, booklists, and activity sheets at the DIY station, along with any materials necessary for completing the activities. Fill the DIY book basket with library materials for browsing or checkout relating to the theme. Creating a corresponding display on a wall or bulletin board is a great way to drum up interest in the DIY station and enhance the theme.

You'll find thematic booklists in each chapter. You can use these as starting points for collecting books for a DIY display or book basket or reproduce them as handouts for patrons. Titles in these booklists are designated as Primary (Preschool through Grade 3), Upper Elementary (Grades 4–7), Teen (Grades 8–12), and Adult. Some specific activity instructions also include short booklists; these are titles that work well with the activity being described.

After they complete their DIY activities, invite patrons to submit an entry in the raffle box. This entry can take two different forms: a completed activity or an entry card. At the end of this introduction you'll find a reproducible basic entry card that can be used with any theme. This is an easy, straightforward way to allow patrons to leave their information and take their completed DIY activities home. Some chapters also include theme-specific reproducible entry cards (known as "I Did a DIY Activity!" cards). The other option is to include spaces for names and telephone numbers (and ages, if desired) on the activity sheets themselves; patrons place the completed sheets in the raffle box. By asking patrons to leave completed activity sheets, librarians have access to answers and feedback. These are useful for creating "Last Month at the DIY Station" compilations of selected responses to include on bookmarks or in the library newsletter. Completed activity sheets also make simple, eye-catching displays on walls or bulletin boards. Be sure to remove any personal patron information, such as full names and telephone numbers, prior to posting projects. Also, when collecting names and phone numbers, it is very important that you protect the privacy and safety of your patrons. Therefore, be sure your raffle box is not left open or placed in a spot where it can be filched or tampered with. A closed and locked box, placed in a location that can be easily supervised by staff, is recommended.

At the end of the month, hold a drawing. The patron whose paper is pulled out of the box wins a prize (often, the prize is related to the monthly theme). Many libraries track program participation statistics, and the submissions in the raffle box serve as a simple way to calculate the number of patrons who have used the DIY station in a given period of time. Due to the independent nature of the DIY station, you can expect an approximate (rather than exact) usage count, understanding that not every patron who visits the DIY station will leave an entry in the raffle box.

PROMOTING YOUR DIY STATION

As with most programs, advertising the DIY station will increase the number of patrons who participate in your library. An article in the local newspaper or the library newsletter can promote awareness of the DIY station. Eye-catching displays and signs directing library visitors to the DIY station will also encourage participation. Each month, consider reporting on the previous month's DIY programming by posting the names of prize winners and selected patron responses. The following is a sample article following up on DIY activities for the month of May.

An Example of a Promotional Article for a Newspaper or Library Newsletter

Last month at the DIY station, we focused on museums. Congratulations to Joe, who won the Crayon Guessing Jar contest (Joe's guess was 158, and there were 162 crayons in the jar).

We also drew a random entry from all of the DIY submissions. Congratulations to Sheila, who won a free pass to the Historical Museum!

We asked patrons to tell us the names and artists of their favorite paintings. Some of the responses were:

The Mona Lisa by Leonardo da Vinci
Great Wave by Katsushika Hokusi
Sunflowers Sunflowers by Vincent van Gogh
White Shell by Georgia O'Keefe

We hope you had a chance to visit our DIY station last month! If you didn't, you can find a list of great books about museums on our Web site. Be sure to visit the DIY station this month for all kinds of fun activities and a chance to win a fabulous prize! The DIY station is located near the hardcover children's fiction and is open to all ages anytime the library is open.

AVOIDING POTENTIAL PITFALLS

DIY programming offers numerous benefits, but be aware of potential harmless pitfalls as well. Because this program is open to the public, expect some misuse of materials. Supplies will likely disappear or be moved around within the library once in awhile, and the staff member who reads the completed activity sheets each month may be surprised by occasional inappropriate responses. Placing the DIY station near an area that is regularly staffed (such as a circulation desk or reference desk) will help alleviate these problems.

REPRODUCIBLES

Reproducible basic raffle entry cards and a welcome sign follow. The sign, placed in an acrylic sign holder, informs and welcomes library visitors to the DIY station.

After completing a DIY activity, fill out this card and drop it in the box for a chance to win a fabulous prize!

I DID A DIY ACTIVITY!

Name: _____

Age: _____

Phone number: _____

The activity I did was:

After completing a DIY activity, fill out this card and drop it in the box for a chance to win a fabulous prize!

I DID A DIY ACTIVITY!

Name: _____

Age: _____

Phone number: _____

The activity I did was:

After completing a DIY activity, fill out this card and drop it in the box for a chance to win a fabulous prize!

I DID A DIY ACTIVITY!

Name: _____

Age: _____

Phone number: _____

The activity I did was:

After completing a DIY activity, fill out this card and drop it in the box for a chance to win a fabulous prize!

I DID A DIY ACTIVITY!

Name: _____

Age: _____

Phone number: _____

The activity I did was:

Welcome to the DIY Station!

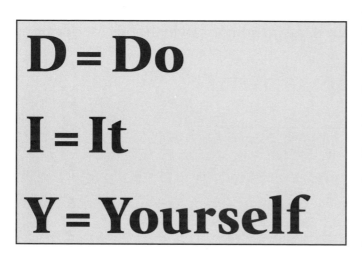

D = Do

I = It

Y = Yourself

Here you will find all kinds of activities to do alone or with friends or family at the library. Everything you need is on this table. Feel free to take materials to another table or area to do the activities. If you have questions, please ask at the Help Desk.

After completing any of our DIY activities, please fill out a card and drop it in the box. We'll draw a name each month for a fabulous prize!

1

January: Fairy Tales

January 4, 1785, is the birth date of Jacob Grimm; and because of the important literary contributions of the Brothers Grimm (Jacob and Wilhelm), January is an ideal time to highlight fairy tales at the DIY station. Of course, fairy tales may be celebrated any time of the year so feel free to present the fairy tale activities when it best suits your library's schedule of events.

Fairy tales hold a very significant place in the world of children's literature. In fact, the impact of their cultural relevance has resulted in many novels and films for children, teens, and adults. In addition, the popularity of the genre has extended into a long list of fractured fairy tales that have been inspired by traditional stories.

The activities and displays presented in this chapter will help highlight the library's selection of traditional fairy tales and works inspired by them. A reproducible page of "I Did a DIY Activity!" slips and a booklist can be found at the end of the chapter.

DISPLAY IDEAS FOR FAIRY TALE FUN

This month's first two activities serve as interactive displays. Activity 1, "My Favorite Fairy Tale Character and Scene," gives kids a great way to share their favorite stories. The display of drawing submissions inspires others to participate and serves as a peer recommendation readers' advisory tool.

Activity 2, "Create a Magic Carpet," results in a colorful display that attracts many and gives you another opportunity to showcase the library's fairy tale collection. It also serves as a nice backdrop to highlight some of your Eastern, Middle Eastern, and non-European fairy tales and folktales, allowing patrons to discover the rich and diverse history of this literary form.

A table featuring books from the library's fairy tale collection creates a simple and attractive display. The impressive art on the covers of many traditional fairy tales makes an eye-catching presentation that attracts many visitors. You may also wish to display accompanying film adaptations. The booklist at the end of the chapter represents a selection of traditional fairy tales, fractured fairy tales, novels inspired by the original tales, and books to help extend the fairy tale experience.

EXTENSIONS ON THE THEME

Fairy tales naturally lend themselves to creative and literary library programs. A fairy tale–themed story time is an obvious extension of this month's activities. As an extended craft activity during story time, participants can create crowns or jewelry. Consider asking local carpeting and flooring stores in your area for carpet-remnant donations. Many businesses are happy to make donations to the library. Use the carpet remnants as "magic carpets" for kids to ride to "fairy tale land." For elementary school-aged children, consider a fractured fairy tale party. The hilarious twists and turns of fractured fairy tales have enormous appeal with this age group.

Reader's theater programs are very popular with 'tweens in the upper-elementary-school age category. The familiarity of traditional fairy tales and the chance to perform make this program a great fit. Simply introduce the story to your participants. Consider putting together a box of accessories and costumes to enhance and inspire the theater experience. Invite guests to watch your fairy tale reader's theater program come to life. 'Tweens usually enjoy the opportunity to perform, and audiences appreciate the live theater opportunity.

Host a medieval or Renaissance fair. As part of the event, invite guests to participate in a potluck fairy tale feast. Jane Yolen's *Fairy Tale Feasts* cookbook series provides many recipes and ideas for your patrons. This event is a terrific community builder. Encourage guests to dress up and consider concluding the event with a costume parade.

A library Lego event is a great way to include library visitors who may not be interested in dressing up and acting out stories. Invite library guests to use Legos to build a castle fit for a fairy tale character. Be sure to take photos of the castles and post them near the DIY station or on the library's Web site.

Include patrons of all ages with a fairy tale film festival. Many fairy tales have made it to the big screen, and many others have been inspired by traditional tales. If your library has a movie license, consider hosting the event as a week-long festival for children, teens, and adults.

Activity 1: My Favorite Fairy Tale Character and Scene

Age Level: Pre-K through Upper Elementary

Activity Time: Varies

What It Is: This is a drawing activity that encourages originality and creativity. It is also a community builder as each participant's contribution adds to the quantity and quality of the display.

How It's Done: Patrons pick up an activity sheet, crayons, and colored pencils at the DIY station. Completed activity sheets are left in a basket for library staff to hang as a part of the display at the DIY station. Patrons are invited to complete an "I Did a DIY Activity!" sheet and place it in the raffle box for a chance to win a prize.

Materials Needed

- Activity sheets
- Crayons or colored pencils
- Patron instruction sheet
- Shallow basket for collecting finished projects

A Few Days Ahead

- Identify wall space near the DIY station to display the artwork.
- Generate activity sheets, or copy the activity sheet included in this chapter.
- Generate instructions, or copy the instructions included in this chapter.

Opening Day

- Display instructions in a clear sign holder or on a wall near the DIY station.
- Place activity sheets, crayons, colored pencils, and a basket for completed "My Favorite Fairy Tale Character and Scene" artwork at the DIY station.

As the Month Progresses

- Add completed activities to the growing display.

Tips and Flourishes

- A book display of traditional fairy tales and fractured fairy tales helps inspire participation. A reproducible booklist is included at the end of this chapter. Make copies for library visitors to pick up.
- For additional creative and open-ended drawing ideas, consider browsing through Susan Striker's *The Anti-Coloring Book* series. The activities presented in these books give children a starting block to help stimulate and encourage imagination and creativity. There are many projects in *The Anti-Coloring Book* series that fit well with the fairy tale theme. "Make Three Wishes on This Magic Lantern" in *The Third Anti-Coloring Book* is one example.

Patron instructions and a reproducible activity sheet follow; feel free to copy or adapt them.

My Favorite Fairy Tale Character and Scene

1. Take an activity sheet.

2. Think of your favorite fairy tale. If you need some ideas, browse through the library's fairy tale collection.

3. Using the crayons and colored pencils provided, draw your favorite character from your favorite fairy tale scene. The setting can be happy, scary, or sad. It's up to you! Write the name of the character and fairy tale at the bottom of your drawing.

4. Leave your drawing in the basket, and we'll hang it up for you.

5. Fill out an "I Did a DIY Activity" sheet and place it in the raffle box for your chance to win a prize.

From *DIY Programming and Book Displays: How to Stretch Your Programming without Stretching Your Budget and Staff* by Amanda Moss Struckmeyer and Svetha Hetzler. Santa Barbara, CA: Libraries Unlimited. Copyright © 2010.

My Favorite Fairy Tale Character and Scene

Name of character and scene:

Activity 2: Create a Magic Carpet

Age Level: Pre-K through Teen

Activity Time: Varies

What It Is: This is an art activity that encourages originality and creativity. Like Activity 1, it is also a community builder as each participant's contribution adds to the quantity and quality of the display.

How It's Done: Patrons pick up an activity sheet, crayons, and colored pencils at the DIY station. Completed activity sheets are left in a basket for library staff to hang as a part of the display at the DIY station. Patrons are invited to complete an "I Did a DIY Activity!" sheet and place it in the raffle box for a chance to win a prize.

Materials Needed

- Standard letter-size copy paper (8½" × 11") or construction paper (9" × 12") in assorted colors
- Crayons or colored pencils
- Patron instruction sheet
- Shallow basket for collecting finished projects

A Few Days Ahead

- Identify wall space near the DIY station to display the "magic carpets."
- Generate instructions, or copy the instructions included in this book.

Opening Day

- Display instructions in a clear sign holder or on a wall near the DIY station.
- Place activity sheets, crayons, colored pencils, and a basket for completed "magic carpets" at the DIY station.

As the Month Progresses

- Add completed activities to the growing display.

Tips and Flourishes

- Instead of paper, supply felt or flannel for an actual fabric version of your "magic carpets." For added interest, consider offering embellishments such as sequins, beads, glitter, fabric markers, and yarn.
- A book display of Oriental rug books and non-European fairy tales such as *Arabian Nights* may encourage participation and give your visitors some design ideas. Browse through your library's 746 section for books on Oriental rugs, or try the titles listed here:

  - Azizollahoff, J.R. *Oriental Rugs from A to Z*. Schiffer, 2004.
  - Blackburn, Mark. *Oriental Rugs: The Secrets Revealed*. Schiffer, 2007.
  - McNaughton, Meik, and Ian McNaughton. *Making Miniature Oriental Rugs and Carpets*. Guild of Master Craftsman Publications, 1998.

Patron instructions follow; feel free to copy or adapt them.

Create a Magic Carpet to Take You Anywhere You Want to Go!

1. Take a piece of paper.

2. Use crayons or colored pencils to create exotic designs.

3. If you'd like, write down the name of a magical or fairy tale land where you would like your carpet to fly.

4. Fill out an "I Did a DIY Activity" sheet and put it in the raffle box for your chance to win a prize.

Activity 3: Create Your Own Fractured Fairy Tale

Age Level: Pre-K through Upper Elementary

Activity Time: 5–10 minutes

What It Is: This is a fill-in-the-blank writing activity similar to Mad Libs, a popular word game where substitution words are inserted to create a humorous story.

How It's Done: Patrons pick up activity sheets and pencils at the DIY station. The blank spaces are filled in to complete the story. Stories may be left in the basket at the DIY station for staff to display. Alternatively, participants may take their stories home. Contributors are invited to complete an "I Did a DIY Activity!" sheet and place it in the raffle box.

Materials Needed

- Patron activity sheets
- Pencils
- Basket for completed stories

A Few Days Ahead

- Generate an activity sheet, or copy the one included in this book. Instructions are included in the activity sheet.

Opening Day

- Set out activity sheets, pencils, and a basket for completed stories at the DIY station.

Tips and Flourishes

- Ask patrons to illustrate their story. Consider providing colored pencils or crayons at the DIY station.
- Suggest working with a partner so that one partner reads only the fill-in-the-blank word choices without reading the rest of the story. Without knowing the context of the story, the end results are always outrageous!
- Ask 'tweens and teens to continue the story or make up their own fill-in-the-blank story.
- Publish completed stories in your library's newsletter.
- Host a fill-in-the-blank story program to give library visitors the opportunity to share their stories.

   Patron instructions and a reproducible activity sheet follow; feel free to copy or adapt them.

Create Your Own Fractured Fairy Tale!
Instructions

Everyone loves reading fractured fairy tales. Here is your chance to write one for others to read. Fill in the blanks by choosing a word from categories A–I. For example, your choice for A would be boy, girl, pig, wolf, or bear. Leave your completed fairy tale in the basket, and we'll post it on the bulletin board. Be sure to fill out an "I Did a DIY Activity" sheet for your chance to win a prize.

Choose a name, object, setting, or activity from each group to create your fractured fairy tale.

A: boy, girl, pig, wolf, bear

B: Jack, Goldilocks, your name, name of your brother, sister, or friend

C: forest, mall, grocery store, library

D: blueberries, underwear, books, cheese doodles

E: the pizzeria, grandma's house, the diner, the café

F: cell phone, Nintendo DS, comic book, lunch box

G: play tag, color

H: skateboard, knit

I: sleeping, howling, tiptoeing, dusting

Create Your Own Fractured Fairy Tale

Once upon a time, there was a little (A) _____ named

(B) _____. (B) _____ loved

to (G or H) _____. One day,

(B) _____ wandered into the (C) _____ and

found some (D) _____. Because

(B) _____ was so excited to find (D) _____,

(B) _____ lost track of time, and it started to get dark. Now

(B) _____ was scared, lost, and hungry. Just then (choose a

different name from group B—it will be B2) _____ jumped

out of the (C) _____ and offered

(B) _____ a ride to (E) _____.

At first (B) _____ was a little suspicious but hunger

won out. (B2) _____ lent (B) _____ a

(F) _____. After getting a bite to eat, the two new friends decided to

(G) _____ and (H) _____. Months have passed

since the two first met and now, the unlikely duo can be found all around town

(I) _____ and (choose another word from

group I) _____.

The End.

Activity 4: Fairy Tale Matching Game

Age Level: Pre-K through Upper Elementary

Activity Time: 5 minutes

What It Is: This is a matching activity. Patrons have a chance to show off their knowledge of traditional tales by matching well-known literary characters to the settings, quotes, and traits that best describe them.

How It's Done: Participants pick up a "Fairy Tale Matching Game" activity sheet, and match the character with their setting, quote, or trait. Patrons are invited to complete an "I Did a DIY Activity!" sheet and place it in the raffle box.

Materials Needed

- Activity sheets
- Pencils

A Few Days Ahead

- Generate activity sheets, or copy the ones included in this book. Instructions for this activity are included in the activity sheet.

Opening Day

- Set out activity sheets and pencils at the DIY station.

Tips and Flourishes

- Consider a matching game for teens in which participants are asked to match the original tale with the novels inspired by them. For example, *Ella Enchanted* would be matched with *Cinderella*.
- Display the books featured on the activity sheets.

    A reproducible activity sheet follows; feel free to copy or adapt it.

Fairy Tale Matching Game

Test your fairy tale knowledge by matching the fairy tale characters on the left with the setting, objects, quotes, or traits on the right. Fill out an "I Did a DIY Activity Sheet" and place it in the raffle box for your chance to win a prize.

Column A	Column B
Goldilocks	Glass slipper
Big Bad Wolf	Beautiful, long hair
Jack	Trip, trap, trip, trap
Rapunzel	Magic beans
Sleeping Beauty	Spinning wheel
Big Billy Goat Gruff	"Run run as fast as you can!"
Rumpelstiltskin	New Year's Eve
Gingerbread Man	"I'll huff and I'll puff . . ."
Little Match Girl	Gold
Cinderella	Porridge

Answer Key for "Fairy Tale Matching Game"

Goldilocks: **Porridge**

Big Bad Wolf: **"I'll huff and I'll puff . . ."**

Jack: **Magic beans**

Rapunzel: **Beautiful, long hair**

Sleeping Beauty: **Spinning wheel**

Big Billy Goat Gruff: **Trip, trap, trip, trap**

Rumpelstiltskin: **Gold**

Gingerbread Man: **"Run run as fast as you can!"**

Little Match Girl: **New Year's Eve**

Cinderella: **Glass slipper**

I Did a DIY Activity!

If you did an activity at the DIY station, please fill out this form and drop it in the ballot box. You might win a fabulous prize!

My name is _____.

I am _____ years old.

My phone number is _____.

Draw a circle around all the activities you did:

My Favorite Fairy Tale Character and Scene

Create a Magic Carpet

Create Your Own Fractured Fairy Tale

Fairy Tale Matching Game

I Did a DIY Activity!

If you did an activity at the DIY station, please fill out this form and drop it in the ballot box. You might win a fabulous prize!

My name is _____.

I am _____ years old.

My phone number is _____.

Draw a circle around all the activities you did:

My Favorite Fairy Tale Character and Scene

Create a Magic Carpet

Create Your Own Fractured Fairy Tale

Fairy Tale Matching Game

Fairy Tales: Traditional Stories and Twisted Tales

Becker, Helaine. *Mother Goose Unplucked: Crazy Comics, Zany Activities, Nutty Facts, and Other Twisted Tales on Childhood Favorites.* Maple Tree Press, 2007. Upper Elementary.

Familiar fairy tales are twisted into outrageous retellings. Includes amusing activities such as exposés, crafts, recipes, riddles, and brainteasers.

Hale, Shannon. *Rapunzel's Revenge.* Bloomsbury, 2008. Teen.

An Old West, graphic-novel retelling of *Rapunzel.*

Lester, Helen. *Tackylocks and the Three Bears.* Houghton Mifflin, 2002. Primary.

Tacky the penguin and his friends perform a play for Mrs. Beakly's class, with Tacky playing the role of Goldilocks.

Levine, Gail Carson. *Ella Enchanted.* Harper Collins, 1997. Teen.

A novel based on the classic tale of *Cinderella.* Ella struggles against her childhood curse of obedience.

Marshall, James. *The Three Little Pigs.* Dial Books for Young Readers, 1989. Primary.

The familiar tale of the Big Bad Wolf, the three little pigs, and their homes made of straw, sticks, and bricks.

McClintock, Barbara. *Cinderella.* Scholastic Press, 2005. Primary.

The traditional story of *Cinderella* is accompanied by McClintock's pen-and-ink and watercolor illustrations.

Pullman, Philip. *Aladdin and the Enchanted Lamp.* Arthur A. Levine Books, 2005. Upper elementary.

A retelling of one of the most famous of the *Arabian Nights* tales. Aladdin, a poor tailor's son, acquires a magic lamp that transforms his life.

Scieszka, Jon. *The True Story of the Three Little Pigs.* Viking Kestral, 1989. Primary.

The wolf gives his outrageous version of what really happened with the three little pigs.

Shah, Tahir. *In Arabian Nights: A Caravan of Moroccan Dreams.* Bantam Books, 2008. Adult.

A journal of travel across Morocco that includes a collection of traditional stories gathered from *A Thousand and One Nights.*

Wilcox, Leah. *Falling for Rapunzel.* G. P. Putnam's Sons, 2003. Primary.

An outlandish fractured adaptation of *Rapunzel,* in which Rapunzel continually misunderstands what the prince is saying.

Zelinsky, Paul O. *Rapunzel.* Dutton Children's Books, 1997. Primary.

The traditional story of *Rapunzel* is accompanied by Zelinsky's powerful oil paintings. Zelinsky's illustrations earned the Caldecott Award.

2

February: Friendship

We Love Books!

February is the perfect time to celebrate friendship and love. Valentine's Day is a widely celebrated holiday that interests individuals of all ages, so this special day is the cornerstone for DIY activities this month. Rather than focusing on romantic love, we use the DIY station to concentrate on love for special books. We also feature a friendship activity, a Valentine fill-in-the-blank story, and a happiness-centered activity inspired by author and illustrator Todd Parr.

DISPLAY IDEAS FOR FRIENDSHIP MONTH

Find or create hearts of all shapes, sizes, and colors to fill your bulletin board and display case this month. Craft stores offer a variety of precut hearts in different colors and sizes. Make your own by using a stencil or die cutter with colored construction paper, patterned scrapbook paper, or gift wrap. If you host a Valentine-making program, add patrons' creations to the display. Be sure to include books with a theme of friendship in the display case and at the DIY station; see the booklist at the end of this chapter for ideas.

An easy, interesting addition to this month's displays are "I Love . . ." lists created by library staff and other community figures. These simple lists are made on pieces of colorful construction paper. Each person writes, "I Love . . ." at the top of a sheet of paper, followed by a bulleted list of a few things close to his or her heart. These might include things as simple as peanut butter sandwiches, sharp pencils, or new shoes. Of course, encourage list makers to include favorite book titles! Finished lists can be posted on bulletin boards or propped inside display cases. Include the name and title of the person who made each list; if time and resources allow, also include a photo of each person alongside the lists.

Because patrons may wish to take their finished projects home or leave them to add to the display, a separate sheet for entering the prize drawing is practical. A reproducible page of "I Did a DIY Activity!" slips is included in this chapter.

EXTENSIONS ON THE THEME

Valentine Making

Patrons of all ages love to make and give Valentines. Gather materials such as doilies, construction paper, wiggle eyes, crayons, stickers, ribbon, and sequins. Provide several samples of different types of Valentines, and let participants get creative with the materials. You'll be surprised at the imaginative ideas they'll come up with!

Valentine Color Scavenger Hunt

Host a scavenger hunt–style program for school-aged children. Provide a list of items they must find in the stacks. For example, your list might include a red book, a pink book, a picture of a heart, a book about friends, a book by an author whose last name begins with the letter V, and so on. If you have access to multiple digital cameras, send teams of older children into the library and have them document their findings by photographing each item on the list. You can also have teams write the title, author, and call number of each book on the list next to the criteria it meets.

BOOKLIST FOR FRIENDSHIP MONTH

You'll find a reproducible booklist at the end of this chapter. Use it as a patron handout or as a starting point for a book display or book basket. Patrons may wish to check these books out or look at them for inspiration while completing DIY activities. Find other friendship- and Valentine-related books in your own collection to include in the display as well; cull from all sections and genres, including picture books, fiction and nonfiction, children's, teen, and adult.

Activity 1: A Valentine for a Book

Age Level: Elementary through Teen

Activity Time: Varies widely, depending on the involvement of the patron

What It Is: In this creative art and literature appreciation activity, patrons are invited to design simple Valentines dedicated to favorite books.

How It's Done: Patrons find activity sheets, pencils, and crayons at the DIY station. Each participant decides on a favorite book to write a Valentine for, then completes the activity sheet according to the instructions. Individuals choose whether to take their Valentines home or leave their projects in the raffle box so that library staff can post them. After completing this activity, each patron is invited to fill out an "I Did a DIY Activity!" slip and place it in the raffle box.

Materials Needed
- Activity sheets
- Patron instructions
- Pencils
- Crayons
- Scissors

A Few Days Ahead
- Photocopy activity sheets.
- Generate instructions, or copy the instructions included in this book.

Opening Day
- Display instructions in a sign holder on the DIY table, or post them on a wall nearby.
- Place activity sheets in an easily accessed place on the table along with pencils, scissors, and crayons.
- You may want to complete an activity sheet and display it at the DIY station as an example.

As the Month Progresses
- Collect activity sheets from the raffle box; post these on a bulletin board or poster near the DIY station.

Tips and Flourishes
- Providing additional art supplies allows library visitors to stretch their creativity. Consider placing magic markers, colored pencils, stickers, and other materials at the DIY station.
- Not only do Valentines make lovely displays, they also make fabulous books! At the end of the month, create a book out of the Valentines by placing each one in a page protector inside a three-ring binder. The binder works best for browsing; if you'd like to have the Valentine book available for checkout, try laminating each Valentine and trimming the film to a uniform rectangular size, then binding these together into a book.

Reproducible patron instructions and an activity sheet follow; feel free to copy or adapt them.

Make a Valentine for a Book!

What is your favorite book?

Tell the world about it by making a Valentine for it!

At the DIY station, you'll find activity sheets and art supplies. Help yourself and follow these steps:

1. Fill in the lines on your Valentine.

2. Decorate your Valentine using the art supplies at the DIY station.

3. Cut out your Valentine.

4. Take your Valentine home or leave it in the raffle box. If you leave your Valentine here, we'll add it to our display!

Be sure to fill out an "I Did a DIY Activity!" slip and place it in the raffle box; you could win a fabulous prize!

A Valentine for a Book

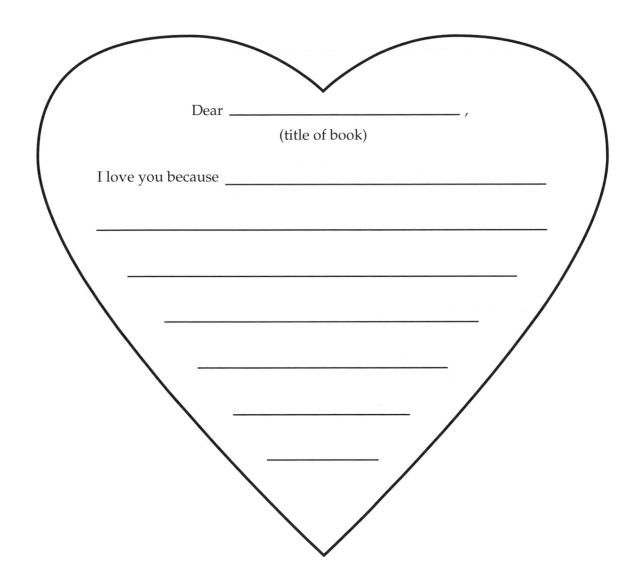

Dear _____ ,

(title of book)

I love you because _____

_____

_____

_____

_____

_____

_____

Activity 2: Things That Make Me Happy

Age Level: Pre-K through Teen

Activity Time: 1–5 minutes

What It Is: In this writing, drawing, and self-awareness activity inspired by author and illustrator Todd Parr, library visitors write and draw items that make them feel happy.

How It's Done: Participants pick up activity sheets, pencils, and crayons at the DIY station. Using Todd Parr's books and images as inspiration, they write or draw (or both) a variety of items that make them feel happy. Individuals choose whether to take their Valentines home or leave their projects in the raffle box so that library staff can post them. After completing this activity, each patron is invited to fill out an "I Did a DIY Activity!" slip and place it in the raffle box.

Materials Needed
- Activity sheets
- Pencils
- Crayons
- Patron instructions
- Todd Parr books, including *Things That Make You Feel Good/Things That Make You Feel Bad*, and images, found in calendars, book catalogs, discarded books, and book jackets

A Few Days Ahead
- Photocopy activity sheets.
- Generate instructions, or copy the instructions included in this book.

Opening Day
- Display instructions in a sign holder on the DIY table, or post them on a wall nearby.
- Place activity sheets in an easily accessed place on the table along with pencils and crayons.
- Display Todd Parr books and images at or near the DIY station.

As the Month Progresses
- Collect activity sheets from the raffle box; post these on a bulletin board or poster near the DIY station.

Tips and Flourishes
- This activity could be made even simpler by posting a large piece of butcher paper on a wall near the DIY station and writing "Things That Make Us Happy" at the top. Patrons are invited to use crayons or magic markers to add one or two items to the list. In the end, you'll be left with a long list of items that make people in your community happy. Consider publishing this in a library newsletter or your local newspaper.
- To enhance this month's display, take pictures of library patrons, staff, or community members smiling. Place these photographs in the display case or add them to the bulletin board. Be sure to get permission before photographing or displaying photographs.

Activity 2: Things That Make Me Happy (*Continued*)

- It is very likely that most of your library's Todd Parr books will be checked out within the first few days of having this activity available. It is worth investing in a calendar or a few posters with Todd Parr images on them to provide inspiration from this author and illustrator even after all of his books are checked out. If your library does not own books by Parr, try substituting titles about friendship or happiness by other authors (see the booklist at the end of this chapter for ideas).

Reproducible patron instructions and an activity sheet follow; feel free to copy or adapt them.

Things That Make Me Happy

Author and illustrator Todd Parr writes a lot about feelings and things that make people feel good.

What makes you happy?

Write or draw some things that make you happy on an activity sheet, found at the DIY station.

Some things you might draw or write on your list are . . .

- Good books
- Favorite foods
- Holidays
- Your favorite color
- Things you like to look at
- Your best friend

When you are finished, take your activity sheet home or leave it in the raffle box so we can put it on display for you. Be sure to fill out an "I Did a DIY Activity!" slip and leave it in the raffle box; you could win a fabulous prize!

From *DIY Programming and Book Displays: How to Stretch Your Programming without Stretching Your Budget and Staff* by Amanda Moss Struckmeyer and Svetha Hetzler. Santa Barbara, CA: Libraries Unlimited. Copyright © 2010.

Things That Make Me Happy

Some things that make me happy are:

_____

_____

_____

_____

_____

_____

_____

_____

_____

_____

_____

Activity 3: Me and My Friend

Age Level: Pre-K through Upper Elementary

Activity Time: 5–10 minutes

What It Is: In this art activity celebrating friends, library guests draw pictures of themselves with their best friends.

How It's Done: At the DIY station, patrons help themselves to activity sheets and art supplies. Each person draws a picture of himself or herself with a best friend. Finished activity sheets are taken home or left in the raffle box to be posted by library staff. Each participant is invited to fill out an "I Did a DIY Activity!" sheet and leave it in the raffle box for a chance to win a prize. Because instructions are included in activity sheets, no separate instruction sheet is necessary.

Materials Needed

- Activity sheets
- Art supplies, such as crayons, magic markers, and colored pencils

A Few Days Ahead

- Photocopy activity sheets.

Opening Day

- Display activity sheets in an easily accessed place on the DIY table along with art supplies.

Tips and Flourishes

- Invite patrons to bring friends to a "Me and My Friend" party. At the party, sing "The More We Get Together," read books about friends, and make friendship bracelets by stringing pony beads onto pipe cleaners.
- At the end of the month, bind activity sheets into a book for browsing or circulation.

   A reproducible activity sheet follows; feel free to copy or adapt it.

Me and My Friend

Who is your best friend? What do you like to do with your friend? Draw a picture of yourself and your friend having fun together. Take your finished project home or leave it in the raffle box for us to add to our display. Be sure to fill out an "I Did a DIY Activity!" slip and leave it in the raffle box; you could win a fabulous prize!

Activity 4: Fill-In Story

Age Level: Upper Elementary through Teen

Activity Time: 5–10 minutes

What It Is: In this silly writing activity, participants fill in blank spaces with specific types of words to finish a story.

How It's Done: Patrons pick up activity sheets and pencils at the DIY station and follow the instructions to complete the story using their own words. Finished projects can be taken home or left in the raffle box to be posted by library staff. Participants are invited to fill out an "I Did a DIY Activity!" slip and place it in the raffle box for a chance to win a prize. Because instructions are included on the activity sheets, no separate instruction sheet is necessary.

Materials Needed

- Activity sheets
- Pencils

A Few Days Ahead

- Photocopy activity sheets.

Opening Day

- Place activity sheets and pencils at the DIY station.

Tips and Flourishes

- At the end of the month, bind activity sheets into a book for circulation or browsing.
- Host a program where attendees write fill-in stories together. They can work in teams to complete one story or work in pairs to alternate choosing words. Participants share their stories and vote to select the zaniest one.
- To assist with this activity, make lists of examples of each part of speech to post near the DIY station.

A reproducible activity sheet follows; feel free to copy or adapt it.

Fill-In Story

Write an original story about you and a friend! First, write a word in each blank in the list below. Be sure to choose words that match the parts of speech specified for each number. Next, copy the words from your list into the story. Finally, read your story from beginning to end. When you are finished, you can take your story home or leave it in the raffle box; at the end of the month, we'll make all of the stories left in the box into a book. Fill out an "I Did a DIY Activity!" slip and leave it in the raffle box for a chance to win a fabulous prize!

1. Noun (a person, place, or thing) _____
2. Color _____
3. Adjective (a word that describes a thing) _____
4. Adjective _____
5. Verb (an action word) _____
6. Verb _____
7. Verb _____
8. Verb _____
9. Adverb (a word that describes an action) _____
10. Feeling _____
11. Feeling _____

My best friend is a (1) _____. My friend is (2) _____,

(3) _____, and (4) _____. My friend and I like to

(5) _____ together. We always (6) _____,

(7) _____, and (8) _____ (9) _____.

When my friend and I are together, I feel (10) _____, and when

my friend has to go home, I feel (11) _____.

From *DIY Programming and Book Displays: How to Stretch Your Programming without Stretching Your Budget and Staff* by Amanda Moss Struckmeyer and Svetha Hetzler. Santa Barbara, CA: Libraries Unlimited. Copyright © 2010.

I Did a DIY Activity!

If you did an activity at the DIY station, please fill out this form and drop it in the raffle box. You might win a fabulous prize!

My name is _____.

I am _____ years old.

My phone number is _____.

The activity I did was:

❐ A Valentine for a Book
❐ Things That Make Me Happy
❐ Me and My Friend
❐ Fill-In Story

I Did a DIY Activity!

If you did an activity at the DIY station, please fill out this form and drop it in the raffle box. You might win a fabulous prize!

My name is _____.

I am _____ years old.

My phone number is _____.

The activity I did was:

❐ A Valentine for a Book
❐ Things That Make Me Happy
❐ Me and My Friend
❐ Fill-In Story

I Did a DIY Activity!

If you did an activity at the DIY station, please fill out this form and drop it in the raffle box. You might win a fabulous prize!

My name is _____.

I am _____ years old.

My phone number is _____.

The activity I did was:

❐ A Valentine for a Book
❐ Things That Make Me Happy
❐ Me and My Friend
❐ Fill-In Story

I Did a DIY Activity!

If you did an activity at the DIY station, please fill out this form and drop it in the raffle box. You might win a fabulous prize!

My name is _____.

I am _____ years old.

My phone number is _____.

The activity I did was:

❐ A Valentine for a Book
❐ Things That Make Me Happy
❐ Me and My Friend
❐ Fill-In Story

From *DIY Programming and Book Displays: How to Stretch Your Programming without Stretching Your Budget and Staff* by Amanda Moss Struckmeyer and Svetha Hetzler. Santa Barbara, CA: Libraries Unlimited. Copyright © 2010.

Friendship Book List

There are lots and lots of books about friends. If you're looking for a few, try these! If you need help finding them, use our online catalog or ask a reference librarian.

Alter, Anna. *Abigail Spells*. Knopf, 2009. Primary.

> George helps his best friend, Abigail, prepare for an upcoming spelling bee. When Abigail makes a mistake, George cheers her up.

Beckery, Bonny. *A Birthday for Bear*. Candlewick, 2009. Primary.

> Bear tries to ignore his birthday, but his friend Mouse is determined to have a celebration.

Cabot, Meg. *Best Friends and Drama Queens*. Scholastic, 2009. Upper Elementary.

> Nine-year-old Allie Finkle has a helpful list of rules. Her list comes in handy when a tough situation arises with a new girl at school.

Child, Lauren. *I Will Be Especially Very Careful*. Dial, 2009. Primary.

> Lola's friend Lotta gets a really special coat, and Lola wants nothing more than to borrow it. Lotta's not sure about lending her new coat, but Lola says that she will be "especially very careful." Will Lola be careful enough to preserve the fluffy whiteness of the coat?

Dowell, Frances O'Roark. *The Kind of Friends We Used to Be*. Atheneum, 2009. Upper Elementary/Teen.

> Twelve-year-olds Kate and Marilyn have been friends since preschool, but they begin to draw further apart as they develop individual interests and find friendship with other people. Sequel to *The Secret Language of Girls* (2004).

Heuvel, Eric. *A Family Secret*. Farrar, Straus, Giroux, 2009. Teen/Adult Graphic Novel.

> Jeroen is looking for yard-sale items in his Dutch grandmother's attic when he finds a scrapbook, which prompts Gran to tell Jeroen about her experiences as a young girl living in Amsterdam during the Holocaust. At that time, Gran's father was a Nazi sympathizer and Esther, Gran's Jewish best friend, disappeared.

Horvath, David. *Just Like Bossy Bear*. Disney Hyperion, 2009. Primary.

> Bossy Bear likes everything to go his way. Things change, though, when Bossy Bear's best friend gives him a taste of his own medicine.

Look, Lenore. *Alvin Ho: Allergic to Camping, Hiking, and Other Natural Disasters*. Schwartz & Wade, 2009. Upper Elementary.

> Alvin's father takes him on a camping trip to develop a love of nature. In the process, Alvin makes a new friend and discovers that, despite his many fears, he can be brave. If you like this one, look for other books about Alvin Ho!

Friendship Book List (*Continued*)

Naylor, Phyllis Reynolds. *Faith, Hope, and Ivy June*. Delacorte, 2009. Upper Elementary/Teen.

> Seventh-graders Ivy June and Catherine participate in a student exchange program and discover that even though their lifestyles, communities, and homes are nothing alike, they have a lot in common.

Willems, Mo. *I Will Surprise My Friend!* Hyperion, 2008. (Look for other books about Elephant and Piggie, too!) Primary.

> Best friends Elephant and Piggie try to surprise one another. The results aren't what you would expect!

3

March: Comics and Graphic Novels

Graphic novels and comics are growing in popularity and variety. Each year, more and more graphic novels are published, making this format accessible to greater numbers of readers. At many libraries, comic books and graphic novels have extremely high circulation rates, indicating their popularity. Featuring comics and graphic novels at the DIY station is a great way to involve patrons who are already passionate about these formats. It also provides a chance for patrons who are not familiar with comics or graphic novels to explore them.

DISPLAY IDEAS FOR COMIC AND GRAPHIC NOVEL MONTH

Many of our DIY activities this month involve finished products, such as drawings of superheroes or original comic strips, that lend themselves well to becoming part of a display. Bulletin boards or wall space will quickly be filled with colorful, imaginative projects; participants will be proud to see their work displayed. We ask patrons to leave completed projects at the DIY station so that library staff can post them. This allows us to quickly review each project to ensure its appropriateness. Posting by library staff is also wise from a safety standpoint, as reaching a bulletin board or other display area often necessitates climbing onto a stool or ladder and using a stapler or thumbtacks.

The American Library Association sells many posters and bookmarks featuring popular comic and graphic novel characters. These are inexpensive and can be used year after year. Discarded book covers also look attractive as part of displays.

Because many of this month's activities may be put on display, a separate sheet for entering the prize drawing is practical. A reproducible page of "I Did a DIY Activity" slips is included in this chapter.

EXTENSIONS ON THE THEME

Look online for Web sites featuring comics and graphic novels. Several interactive comic creation sites are listed in Activity 1, and most authors and illustrators have Web sites. Consider adding links to these sites to the library's Web site.

A superhero party is fun for patrons of all ages. Participants are invited to dress as superheroes, and activities include stretches, power snacks (celery sticks spread with peanut butter or cheese spread is a healthy snack children can help prepare; be aware of food allergies, of course!), and making capes (ask each participant to bring one yard of fabric, which could be purchased or repurposed from an old sheet or curtain, to transform into a decorated cape using glitter, rickrack, fabric paint, and other materials).

Consider hosting a graphic novel book club. Many books are now available in both conventional format and graphic novel format, including The Baby-Sitters Club, The Hardy Boys, and Nancy Drew. Patrons may enjoy reading one title in both formats and comparing the two.

BOOKLIST FOR COMIC AND GRAPHIC NOVEL MONTH

A reproducible booklist is located at the end of this chapter. Use it as a patron handout or as a starting point for a book display or basket. Patrons may wish to check these books out or look at them for inspiration while completing DIY activities. Obviously, the comic and graphic novel sections of the library are brimming with great books for the DIY basket this month. Be sure to include books that appeal to younger readers and older ones. In addition to graphic novels and comics, which are not included on this chapter's booklist, look for nonfiction titles *about* these formats, including author/ illustrator biographies and drawing instruction books.

Activity 1: Complete a Con

Age Level: Elementary through Teen

Activity Time: 5–10 minutes

What It Is: This is a drawing and writing activity. Participa
finished comic strips, and they complete the strips with d

How It's Done: Patrons pick up "Complete a Comic" acti
station, along with pencils and other art supplies (option
contains three panels of a comic strip, two of which ar
which is blank. Each participant fills in the third panel
then submits the finished strip to the raffle box. Library staff collects completed
activity sheets from the box and posts them on a wall or bulletin board near the
DIY station. Each patron is invited to complete an "I Did a DIY Activity" sheet
and place it in the raffle box.

Materials Needed

- Activity sheets
- Pencils
- Crayons or colored pencils (optional)
- Patron instructions

A Few Days Ahead

- Photocopy activity sheets.
- Generate instructions, or copy the instructions included in this book.

Opening Day

- Display instructions in a sign holder on the DIY table, or post them or on a wall
  nearby.
- Place activity sheets, pencils, and other art supplies at the DIY station.

As the Month Progresses

- Collect finished activity sheets from the raffle box and display them.

Tips and Flourishes

- Consider completing one or two comic strips ahead of time to put on display to help
  patrons understand the activity.
- If resources allow, create multiple "Complete the Comic" activity sheets featuring various characters, settings, and situations. For an added challenge, provide the final two
  panels of the comic, and leave the first one blank for patrons to fill in. Comic strips can
  be drawn or generated on a computer. Use a word processing program with drawing
  options, or try Web sites such as pixton.com, stripcreator.com, or readwritethink.org/
  materials/comic.
- At the end of the month, bind completed comic strips into a book for circulation or in-
  library browsing.

Reproducible patron instructions and an activity sheet follow; feel free to copy or adapt them.

Complete a Comic

At the DIY station, you'll find an unfinished comic strip. It's up to you to finish it!

1. Take a pencil and a "Complete a Comic" sheet from the DIY table.

2. Read the first two panels of the comic strip.

3. Decide what should happen next.

4. Fill in the final panel to finish the comic strip.

5. Place your completed sheet in the raffle box. We'll hang it up for you!

6. Fill out an "I Did a DIY Activity" slip and enter it in the raffle box for a chance to win a fabulous prize!

Complete a Comic

Activity 2: Say What?

Age Level: Early Elementary through Teen

Activity Time: 5–10 minutes

What It Is: This is a short creative writing activity in which participants write dialogue between two characters in a comic strip. Optionally, this may also be an art activity, as patrons may color and add illustrations to the comic strip.

How It's Done: Patrons find "Say What?" activity sheets, pencils, and other art supplies (optional) at the DIY station. The activity sheets contain comic strips with characters and speech bubbles but no words. Patrons write the dialogue into the speech bubbles and, if desired, color the characters and draw backgrounds or scenery. Finished activity sheets are placed in the raffle box, and staff hangs them up for display on a wall or bulletin board near the DIY station. Patrons are invited to complete an "I Did a DIY Activity" sheet and place it in the raffle box.

Materials Needed

- Activity sheets
- Patron instructions
- Pencils
- Crayons
- Colored pencils or other art supplies (optional)

A Few Days Ahead

- Photocopy activity sheets.
- Generate instructions, or copy the instructions included in this book.

Opening Day

- Display instructions in a sign holder on the DIY table, or post them on a wall nearby.
- Place activity sheets, pencils, and other art supplies at the DIY station.

As the Month Progresses

- Collect finished activity sheets from the raffle box and display them.

Tips and Flourishes

- Consider completing one or two "Say What?" activity sheets ahead of time to put on display to help patrons understand the activity. If resources allow, create multiple "Say What?" activity sheets featuring various characters. For an added challenge, add more characters or additional panels to the activity sheets.
- Comic strips can be drawn or generated on a computer. Use a word processing program with drawing options, or try Web sites such as pixton.com, stripcreator.com, or readwritethink.org/materials/comic.
- At the end of the month, bind completed activity sheets into a book for circulation or in-library browsing.

Reproducible patron instructions and an activity sheet follow; feel free to copy or adapt them.

Say What?

At the DIY station, you'll find a comic strip. The characters in the strip are talking to one another, but the words are missing! It's up to you to decide what the characters are saying.

1. Take a pencil and a "Say What?" sheet from the DIY table.

2. Look at the comic strip, and decide what the characters are saying.

3. Fill in the speech bubbles to finish the comic strip. If you like, use crayons to color the characters and scenery.

4. Place your completed sheet in the raffle box. We'll hang it up for you!

5. Fill out an "I Did a DIY Activity" slip and enter it in the raffle box for a chance to win a fabulous prize!

Activity 3: Draw a Comic Strip

Age Level: Early Elementary through Teen

Activity Time: 5–10 minutes

What It Is: This is a creative drawing and writing activity in which library visitors generate original comic strips.

How It's Done: Patrons pick up activity sheets, pencils, and crayons (optional) at the DIY station. They create comic strips by drawing and writing in the boxes on the sheets. Finished activity sheets are placed in the raffle box, and staff hangs them up on a wall or bulletin board near the DIY station. Each participant is invited to complete an "I Did a DIY Activity" sheet and place it in the raffle box.

Materials Needed

- Activity sheets
- Pencils
- Crayons (optional)

A Few Days Ahead

- Generate activity sheets, or copy the one included in this book.

Opening Day

- Place activity sheets, pencils, and crayons at the DIY station. No separate instructions are needed.

Tips and Flourishes

- Create a poster of comic strips from the newspaper to give patrons ideas and inspiration. Ask library staff to create comic strips to add to the poster. Hang this poster near the DIY station.
- Provide several different comic strip templates with a variety of numbers of panels. These can be generated quickly with a word processing program.
- At the end of the month, bind completed activity sheets into a book for circulation or in-library browsing.

A reproducible activity sheet follows; feel free to copy or adapt it.

Draw a Comic Strip

Draw your own comic strip! Fill the boxes below with characters, speech or thought bubbles, and other things that will tell a short, funny story. When you are finished, put your strip in the raffle box; we'll post it for you! Be sure to fill out an "I Did a DIY Activity" sheet and place it in the raffle box!

From *DIY Programming and Book Displays: How to Stretch Your Programming without Stretching Your Budget and Staff* by Amanda Moss Struckmeyer and Svetha Hetzler. Santa Barbara, CA: Libraries Unlimited. Copyright © 2010.

Activity 4: Favorite Superpowers

Age Level: Preschool through Teen

Activity Time: 5–10 minutes

What It Is: This is an imaginative voting exercise. Library visitors are asked to indicate which superpowers they would like to have by voting and (optionally) writing answers. Answers are tallied and posted so that the library community can see which superpowers are the most popular.

How It's Done: Patrons pick up voting sheets and pencils at the DIY station. Each person votes on his or her three favorite superpowers, with the option of writing in powers that are not on the list. Voting sheets are submitted to the ballot box along with "I Did a DIY Activity" sheets. At the end of the month, library staff tallies the results and posts them on a poster or bulletin board or on the library's Web site.

Materials Needed
- Voting sheets
- Pencils
- Patron instructions

A Few Days Ahead
- Photocopy and cut voting sheets.
- Generate instructions, or photocopy the instructions included in this book.

Opening Day
- Place voting sheets, pencils, and patron instructions at the DIY station.

Tips and Flourishes
- To foster enthusiasm, collect voting sheets every few days and keep a running tally throughout the month. A bar graph works well for displaying these results. Here is an example:

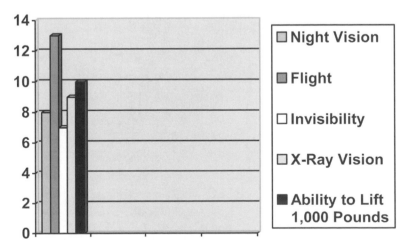

Results from favorite superpowers voting activity.

    Reproducible patron instructions and voting sheets follow; feel free to copy or adapt them.

Vote for Your Favorite Superpower!

Would you like to be able to fly? How about jump over a building? Let's find out what our library's favorite superpowers are!

At the DIY station, you'll find voting sheets and pencils. Please vote by marking your three favorite superpowers. If one of your favorites is not on the list, please add it!

Submit your sheet to the raffle box. We'll tally the answers and let you know which superpowers came out on top!

After you vote, please fill out an "I Did a DIY Activity" sheet and place it in the raffle box for your chance to win a fabulous prize!

Favorite Superpowers Ballots

Vote for Your Favorite Superpowers!

Please mark the three powers on this list that you would most like to have. If your favorite isn't on the list, please add it by writing it on the line.

___ Flight   ___ Invisibility

___ X-Ray Vision   ___ Jumping over buildings

___ Lifting 1,000 pounds   ___ Running 300 miles per hour

___ Speed reading   ___ Mind reading

___ Other (please write) _____

_____

Vote for Your Favorite Superpowers!

Please mark the three powers on this list that you would most like to have. If your favorite isn't on the list, please add it by writing it on the line.

___ Flight   ___ Invisibility

___ X-Ray Vision   ___ Jumping over buildings

___ Lifting 1,000 pounds   ___ Running 300 miles per hour

___ Speed reading   ___ Mind reading

___ Other (please write) _____

_____

Vote for Your Favorite Superpowers!

Please mark the three powers on this list that you would most like to have. If your favorite isn't on the list, please add it by writing it on the line.

___ Flight   ___ Invisibility

___ X-Ray Vision   ___ Jumping over buildings

___ Lifting 1,000 pounds   ___ Running 300 miles per hour

___ Speed reading   ___ Mind reading

___ Other (please write) _____

_____

Vote for Your Favorite Superpowers!

Please mark the three powers on this list that you would most like to have. If your favorite isn't on the list, please add it by writing it on the line.

___ Flight   ___ Invisibility

___ X-Ray Vision   ___ Jumping over buildings

___ Lifting 1,000 pounds   ___ Running 300 miles per hour

___ Speed reading   ___ Mind reading

___ Other (please write) _____

_____

Activity 5: Design a Superhero

Age Level: Pre-K through Teen

Activity Time: 5–10 minutes

What It Is: This is an imaginative art and short writing activity in which participants design unique superheroes.

How It's Done: Library visitors pick up "Design a Superhero" activity sheets at the DIY station, along with pencils and other art supplies. To complete the activity, each participant draws a superhero and writes briefly about him or her. Finished activity sheets are placed in the raffle box, and staff hangs them up on a wall or bulletin board near the DIY station. After completing this activity, each patron is invited to complete an "I Did a DIY Activity" sheet and place it in the raffle box.

Materials Needed

- Activity sheets
- Patron instructions
- Pencils
- Crayons or colored pencils

A Few Days Ahead

- Photocopy activity sheets.
- Generate instructions, or copy the instructions included in this book.

Opening Day

- Display instructions in a sign holder at the DIY station or on a wall nearby.
- Place activity sheets, pencils, and other art supplies at the DIY station.

As the Month Progresses

- Collect finished activity sheets from the raffle box and display them.

Tips and Flourishes

- Consider completing one or two activity sheets ahead of time to put on display.
- If resources allow, provide precut paper shapes and glue sticks for patrons to use to build their superheroes. For example, a circle could become a head, and a rectangle could become a torso.
- At the end of the month, bind completed activity sheets into a book for circulation or in-library browsing.

Reproducible patron instructions and an activity sheet follow; feel free to copy or adapt them.

Instructions for Design a Superhero!

This is your chance to design the ultimate superhero! What powers will he or she have? What will your superhero look like?

1. Take a Design a Superhero sheet, a pencil, and other drawing supplies from the DIY station.

2. Think about what type of superhero you'd like to design.

3. Draw your superhero in the box on the sheet.

4. Place your completed sheet in the raffle box. We'll hang it up for you!

5. Fill out an "I Did a DIY Activity" slip and enter it in the raffle box for a chance to win a fabulous prize!

From DIY Programming and Book Displays: How to Stretch Your Programming without Stretching Your Budget and Staff by Amanda Moss Struckmeyer and Svetha Hetzler. Santa Barbara, CA: Libraries Unlimited. Copyright © 2010.

Design A Superhero!

Below, draw a picture of a superhero you would like to invent. What kinds of special powers will you give your superhero?

My superhero's name is _____.

My superhero's special powers are _____.

From *DIY Programming and Book Displays: How to Stretch Your Programming without Stretching Your Budget and Staff* by Amanda Moss Struckmeyer and Svetha Hetzler. Santa Barbara, CA: Libraries Unlimited. Copyright © 2010.

I Did a DIY Activity!

If you did an activity at the DIY station, please fill out this form and drop it in the ballot box. You might win a fabulous prize!

My name is _____.

I am _____ years old.

My phone number is _____.

The activity I did was:

❐ Complete a Comic
❐ Say What?
❐ Draw a Comic Strip
❐ Favorite Superpowers (Voting)
❐ Design a Superhero

I Did a DIY Activity!

If you did an activity at the DIY station, please fill out this form and drop it in the ballot box. You might win a fabulous prize!

My name is _____.

I am _____ years old.

My phone number is _____.

The activity I did was:

❐ Complete a Comic
❐ Say What?
❐ Draw a Comic Strip
❐ Favorite Superpowers (Voting)
❐ Design a Superhero

I Did a DIY Activity!

If you did an activity at the DIY station, please fill out this form and drop it in the ballot box. You might win a fabulous prize!

My name is _____

I am _____ years old.

My phone number is _____

The activity I did was:

❐ Complete a Comic
❐ Say What?
❐ Draw a Comic Strip
❐ Favorite Superpowers (Voting)
❐ Design a Superhero

I Did a DIY Activity!

If you did an activity at the DIY station, please fill out this form and drop it in the ballot box. You might win a fabulous prize!

My name is _____

I am _____ years old.

My phone number is _____

The activity I did was:

❐ Complete a Comic
❐ Say What?
❐ Draw a Comic Strip
❐ Favorite Superpowers (Voting)
❐ Design a Superhero

From *DIY Programming and Book Displays: How to Stretch Your Programming without Stretching Your Budget and Staff* by Amanda Moss Struckmeyer and Svetha Hetzler. Santa Barbara, CA: Libraries Unlimited. Copyright © 2010.

Booklist for Comic and Graphic Novel Month

You'll find plenty of graphic novels and comics in the stacks! Ask a librarian to point out the graphic novel section to you. Try the following books if you're interested in reading *about* comics or graphic novels.

8fish. *Making Faces: Drawing Expressions for Comics and Cartoons*. Impact Books, 2008. Teen/Adult.

> This manual for drawing expressive faces is useful for beginners and advanced artists.

Abel, Jessica. *Drawing Words, Writing Pictures*. First Second, 2008. Teen/Adult.

> An independent-study course on creating comics. Includes material on storytelling, lettering, layout, and more.

The DC Comics Encyclopedia: The Definitive Guide to the Characters of the DC Universe. DK Publishing, 2008. Teen/Adult.

> Learn in-depth details on DC Comics characters.

Fairrington, Brian. *Drawing Cartoons and Comics for Dummies*. For Dummies, 2009. Teen/Adult.

> The beginner's no-fail guide to comic illustration.

Hamilton, Sue L. *Jack Kirby: Creator and Artist*. ABDO, 2007. Primary/Upper Elementary.

> An introductory biography on Jack Kirby, the "King of Comics."

Hamilton, Sue L. *Joe Sinnott: Artist and Inker*. ABDO, 2007. Primary/Upper Elementary.

> An introductory biography on Joe Sinnott, an artist for Marvel Comics.

Hart, Christopher. *Drawing the New Adventure Cartoons: Cool Spies, Evil Guys and Action Heroes*. Chris Hart Books/Sixth & Spring Books, 2008. Primary/Upper Elementary/Teen.

> Learn to draw your favorite—or least favorite!—characters from video games, comics, and cartoons.

Krensky, Stephen. *Comic Book Century: The History of American Comic Books*. Twenty-First Century Books, 2008. Teen/Adult.

> Explore the history of comic books in America throughout the twentieth century, including cultural influences and an epilogue about comics in the early twenty-first century.

Schmitz, Diane Ridley. *Cartoon Magic*. North Light Books, 2001. Primary/Upper Elementary.

> Introductory-level drawing instruction and tips on how to create great comic strips and posters.

Williams, Freddie E. *The DC Comics Guide to Digitally Drawing Comics*. Watson-Guptill Publications, 2009. Teen/Adult.

> How do they create those amazing special effects in digital comics? Find out in this book!

4

April: Poetry

April is National Poetry Month! Celebrate with a variety of poetry-related activities at the DIY station. This is also a perfect time to highlight the library's poetry collection. A display near the DIY station will likely spark interest in the collection and in the DIY station itself. Patrons of all ages will be drawn to poetry-related books and activities. Some may be surprised at the diversity of topics found in the poetry collection. Be sure to include a mix of creative activities to appeal to as many patrons as possible. And remember, just because April is Poetry Month doesn't mean the DIY station needs to be limited to writing activities!

DISPLAY IDEAS FOR POETRY MONTH

April is the perfect time to celebrate the loveliness of words. Simply writing interesting-sounding words on posters or bulletin boards in different colors and styles makes a unique display or backdrop. Words can also be typed in a word processing program, edited to change the font, size, and color, and printed for posting. Many poetry books have lovely covers, lending themselves well to being part of a display. Be ready to replenish books on display, though; they may be quickly chosen for checkout!

Patrons are often interested in poets and authors, so if resources allow, consider purchasing a poster or two featuring famous poets to hang for display. Poets who appeal to both children and adults, such as Shel Silverstein, are recommended. Poems themselves can easily become part of a display in a case or on a wall. Poems may be cut from discarded books, then put in frames (which can be purchased inexpensively at secondhand shops) and hung or propped up. Word mobiles are easy to create and fun to look at. Simply write 5–10 favorite words on cardstock using different colors, then cut each word out and attach it to a wire coat hanger using fishing line or ribbon.

EXTENSIONS ON THE THEME

If word mobiles are part of the library's décor for April, a mobile-making workshop will be a popular event. Ask patrons to bring a wire hanger; the library supplies cardstock, crayons, scissors, and ribbon or fishing line. Participants choose words they want to include in their mobiles, write the words, cut them out, and attach them to the hangers. This is a simple, enjoyable way to get patrons engaged in words and poetry.

An open mic night or poetry jam will encourage patrons to share original poetry or read a favorite poem aloud. A poetry book can be generated by asking patrons to submit original poetry. Most office-supply stores bind books inexpensively. If resources allow, consider making a copy for each contributor, as well as one to circulate.

Because patrons may wish to take their finished poems and other projects home, a separate sheet for entering the prize drawing is practical. A reproducible page of "I Did a DIY Activity!" slips is included in this chapter.

BOOKLIST FOR POETRY MONTH

You'll find a reproducible booklist at the end of this chapter. You can use it as a patron handout or as a starting point for your book display or book basket. Patrons may wish to check these books out or look at them for inspiration while completing DIY activities. Find other poetry-related books in your own collection to include in the display as well; cull from all sections and genres, including picture books, fiction and nonfiction, children's, teen, and adult.

Activity 1: 24-Hour Poem

Age Level: Elementary through Teen

Activity Time: 5–10 minutes

What It Is: This is a reflective writing activity. Each participant writes a list of 24 words. Each word tells (briefly) what the individual does during each hour of the day.

How It's Done: Patrons pick up "24-Hour Poem" activity sheets at the DIY station, along with pencils. The activity sheet contains prompts to help patrons complete the poem. Completed activity sheets may be taken home (if the library is creating an original poetry book, give patrons the option to leave their activity sheets). Patrons submit "I Did a DIY Activity!" slips to the raffle box.

Materials Needed
- Activity sheets
- Pencils
- Patron instructions

A Few Days Ahead
- Photocopy activity sheets.
- Generate instructions, or copy the instructions included in this book.

Opening Day
- Display instructions in a sign holder or on a wall near the DIY station.
- Place activity sheets and pencils at the DIY station.

Tips and Flourishes
- Ask prominent members of the community, such as teachers and government officials, to complete 24-hour poems. This will provide patrons with a sneak peek at what these people do in a typical day. Try to find some community members whose jobs involve odd hours, such as firefighters and bakers, to write poems. Display these poems to highlight the DIY station this month.
- Include crayons or other art supplies at the DIY station so that patrons can illustrate their 24-hour poems.

Reproducible patron instructions and an activity sheet follow; feel free to copy or adapt them.

24-Hour Poem

What do you do all day? Tell the world about it with a 24-hour poem!

Starting at midnight, write down one word that describes what you do each hour during a typical day. It may be hard to come up with just one word for each hour, but remember that this will give readers a peek at your life, not a full description of everything you do.

Here is an example of a 24-hour poem:

AROUND THE CLOCK WITH AMANDA

Sleep

Sleep

Sleep

Sleep

Sleep

Sleep

Waaaaaake

Hurry!

Work

Work

Work

Work

Eat

Work

Work

Work

Work

Bus

Relax

Read

Talk

Laugh

Sleep

Sleep

When you're finished, take your poem home. Be sure to fill out an "I Did a DIY Activity!" slip and place it in the raffle box; you could win a fabulous prize!

From *DIY Programming and Book Displays: How to Stretch Your Programming without Stretching Your Budget and Staff* by Amanda Moss Struckmeyer and Svetha Hetzler. Santa Barbara, CA: Libraries Unlimited. Copyright © 2010.

24-Hour Poem

Title: _____

By: _____

Write one word describing what you do during each hour of the day.

Time of Day	What You Do
Midnight–1:00 A.M.	
1:00–2:00 A.M.	
2:00–3:00 A.M.	
3:00–4:00 A.M.	
4:00–5:00 A.M.	
5:00–6:00 A.M.	
6:00–7:00 A.M.	
7:00–8:00 A.M.	
8:00–9:00 A.M.	
9:00–10:00 A.M.	
10:00–11:00 A.M.	
11:00 A.M.–Noon	
Noon–1:00 A.M.	
1:00–2:00 A.M.	
2:00–3:00 A.M.	
3:00–4:00 A.M.	
4:00–5:00 A.M.	
5:00–6:00 A.M.	
6:00–7:00 A.M.	
7:00–8:00 A.M.	
8:00–9:00 A.M.	
9:00–10:00 A.M.	
10:00–11:00 A.M.	
11:00 A.M.–Midnight	

Congratulations! You have written a 24-hour poem!

Read your poem by reading the list of words you wrote.

Activity 2: Illustrate a Poem

Age Level: Pre-K through Teen

Activity Time: 5–10 minutes

What It Is: This is a creative art activity. Using published poems as an inspiration, participants draw original illustrations.

How It's Done: Each library guest picks up an "Illustrate a Poem" activity sheet, crayons or colored pencils or markers, and a book of poetry at the DIY station. After selecting and reading one poem from the book, the patron uses the art supplies to create an original illustration for the poem. Completed activity sheets can be taken home, and participants are invited to submit an "I Did a DIY Activity!" slip to the raffle box for a chance to win a prize. Alternatively, completed activity sheets may be left at the DIY station and posted by library staff for a colorful display.

Materials Needed

- Activity sheets
- Pencils
- Crayons, colored pencils, or markers

A Few Days Ahead

- Photocopy activity sheets.

Opening Day

- Place activity sheets, pencils, and art supplies at the DIY station.

Tips and Flourishes

- If time permits, complete a few activity sheets ahead of time to post as examples.
- Plan a related program for older children, in which the librarian reads a poem aloud and children illustrate it. Classical music may help participants feel inspired. As children finish their illustrations, post them around the program area as a mini-museum for browsing.

   A reproducible activity sheet follows; feel free to copy or adapt it.

Illustrate a Poem

In the DIY basket, there are lots of poetry books. Look through the books to find a poem that appeals to you. Then draw a picture to go with the poem. Take your picture home with you and show it to a friend or family member! Be sure to fill out an "I Did a DIY Activity!" slip and put it in the raffle box for your chance to win a fabulous prize!

The poem I am illustrating is called _____.

The poem I am illustrating was written by _____.

Activity 3: Repurposed-Book Poem

Age Level: Upper Elementary through Teen

Activity Time: 10–15 minutes

What It Is: This is a collaborative, ecological, and creative art and writing activity that allows library visitors to transform a discarded book into original poetry. All patrons use the same discarded book, so the end result is one volume of poetry.

How It's Done: At the DIY station, patrons find instructions, pencils, crayons, index cards, clear tape, and a discarded book. Each person selects a page of the book to transform into a poem, then uses the supplies at the DIY station to do so. The book is left at the DIY station, and participants are invited to fill out "I Did a DIY Activity!" slips for entry into the prize drawing.

Materials Needed

- Patron instructions
- A discarded book (paperbacks work well because of their compact size), marked clearly to avoid confusion
- Pencils
- Crayons
- Index cards, sized to fit over the text on one page of the discarded book
- Clear tape

A Few Days Ahead

- Generate instructions, or copy the ones included in this book.
- Complete a few poems in the discarded book as examples.

Opening Day

- Display instructions in a clear sign holder or on a wall near the DIY station.
- Place all other supplies at the DIY station. Include a sample repurposed-book poem, or a photograph of one, to enhance the instructions.

Tips and Flourishes

- This activity is fun to do with groups of 'tweens or teens; give each participant a discarded book and ask everyone to write their names on the front covers. The books are passed around the room, and each participant writes one poem in each book. At the end of the program, each patron takes home the book with his or her name on it, full of poems.
- This is a great activity to highlight on or around Earth Day (April 22).

Patron instructions follow; feel free to copy or adapt them.

Repurposed-Book Poem

With this poem, we'll be giving new life to a book that was headed to the recycling bin! At the DIY station, there is a paperback book with a bright pink "Poems" note on the front. We are transforming this book, which was going to be thrown away, into a book of poetry!

1. Choose a page in the book. Find one with plenty of fun words on it; these are the words you'll use in your poem.

2. Using a crayon, circle some words on the page. You might choose to find words that somehow work together or sound good with one another. It's up to you! You can circle any number of words; for your first repurposed-book poem, try finding between 12 and 15 words.

3. When you are finished circling words, use a darker crayon to color over the words that are not circled. It's okay if you can still see these words through the crayon. Choose several colors for this if you like; try creating a pattern with the colors.

4. Take an index card and a pencil from the DIY station. Write all of the words you circled on the index card, forming your poem. The lines of your poem can be as long or as short as you like.

5. Tape the index card into the book, directly across from the page where you found the words for the poem. Congratulations! You have written a repurposed-book poem!

6. Leave the book at the DIY station for others to write in. Fill out an "I Did a DIY Activity!" slip and leave it in the raffle box for your chance to win a fabulous prize!

Activity 4: Shape Poem

Age Level: Pre-K through Elementary

Activity Time: 5–10 minutes

What It Is: This is a creative writing activity. Library visitors write poems in a variety of shapes, to which the words and phrases in the poems correspond.

How It's Done: Library guests pick up shape templates at the DIY station, along with pencils. Each template holds one large shape, which patrons fill with words and phrases that correspond with that shape. For example, if someone chooses a triangle template, her poem might include items such as "birthday hat," "slice of pizza," and "traffic cone" (items that are shaped like triangles). Finished poems are taken home (if the library is creating an original poetry book, give participants the option to leave their activity sheets). Patrons submit "I Did a DIY Activity!" slips to the raffle box.

Materials Needed

- Photocopied shape templates
- Pencils
- Patron instructions

A Few Days Ahead

- Generate shape templates, or copy the ones included in this book.
- Generate instructions, or copy the instructions included in this book.

Opening Day

- Display instructions in a clear sign holder or on a wall near the DIY station.
- Place shape templates and pencils at the DIY station.

Tips and Flourishes

- Include a few shape-related books in the DIY basket. Early books about shapes often feature a wide variety of items in a certain shape, so these are helpful for finding ideas.
- Include crayons or other art supplies at the DIY station so that patrons can illustrate their shape poems.

Reproducible patron instructions and shape templates follow; feel free to copy or adapt them.

Shape Poem

A shape poem is exactly what it sounds like: a poem written in a certain shape. But these poems don't just look like shapes; they're also about shapes!

1. Choose a shape you'd like to use to guide your poem. Select one of the shapes we've provided, or draw your own.

2. Think of lots of different items that are shaped like the shape you choose. For example, if you choose a circle, think of all the circular things you can. Instead of writing the items you think of in a list, write them inside the shape. Here is an example, using a circle:

CIRCLE POEM

Pizza Cookies

Basketball Plate

Wheel Orange Smiley

Face Baseball Sun

Moon Apple Pie Button

Polka Dot Birthday

Ring Donut Bagel

Clocks

3. Take your poem home and share it! Be sure to fill out an "I Did a DIY Activity!" slip and place it in the raffle box for a chance to win a fabulous prize!

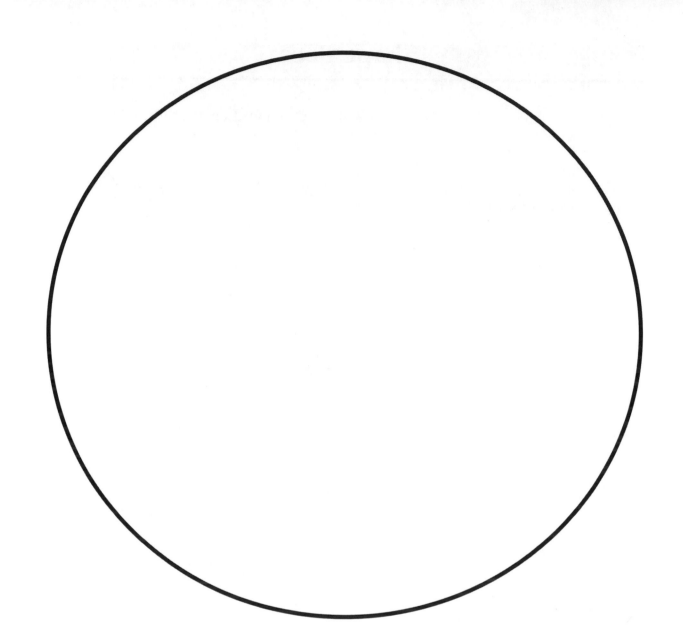

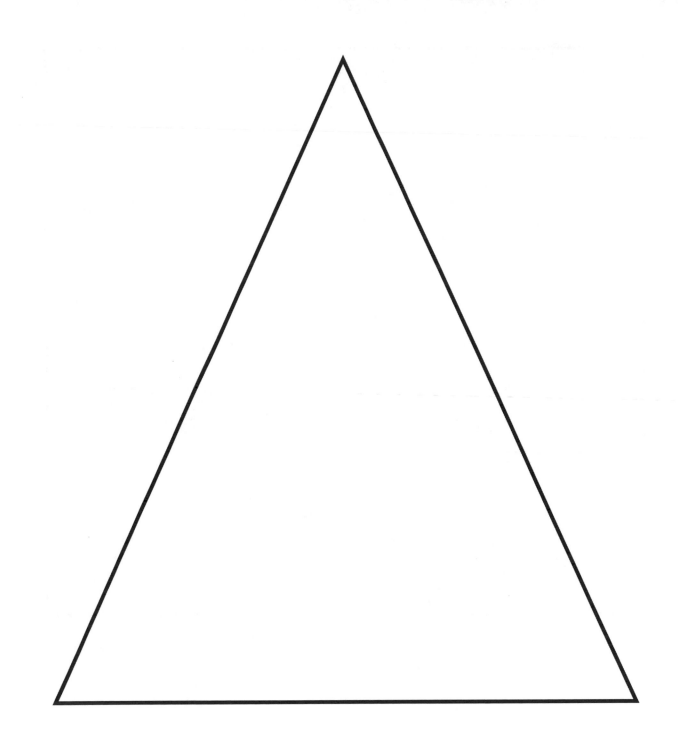

Activity 5: Acrostic Poem

Age Level: Pre-K through Upper Elementary

Activity Time: 5–10 minutes

What It Is: This is a creative writing activity. Patrons use the letters in their names to write acrostic poems.

How It's Done: Library visitors pick up blank writing paper and pencils at the DIY station and complete acrostic poems according to the instructions. Finished poems may be taken home (if the library is creating an original poetry book, give patrons the option to leave their poems). Participants submit "I Did a DIY Activity!" slips to the raffle box.

Materials Needed

- Blank writing paper (lined or unlined)
- Pencils
- Patron instruction sheet

A Few Days Ahead

- Generate instructions, or copy the instructions included in this book.

Opening Day

- Display instructions in a clear sign holder or on a wall near the DIY station.
- Place blank paper and pencils at the DIY station.

Tips and Flourishes

- Create a large acrostic poem, featuring the name of the library, to display on a wall or bulletin board.
- The instructions included in this book direct patrons to use their names as the base for these poems. As an extension, encourage patrons (either in the instructions or in a program) to use other words, such as favorite foods or places, as base words for their poems.
- Include crayons or other art supplies at the DIY station so that patrons can illustrate their acrostic poems.

  Patron instructions follow; feel free to copy or adapt them.

Acrostic Poem

Have fun writing an acrostic poem today! On a sheet of paper, write the letters of your first or last name going down the left-hand side of the page. For example, if your first or last name were Middleton, your page would look like this:

M

I

D

D

L

E

T

O

N

Next, think of a word that describes you, or something you enjoy, that begins with each letter. If you have an M in your name, you might choose the word *magical, musical,* or *mysterious* to describe you, or a word such as *moose, munching,* or *mints* if those are things you enjoy. Write each word going across your paper, like so:

Munching

I

D

D

L

E

T

O

N

Acrostic Poem (*Continued*)

Keep working down the page, adding a word for each letter in your name. In the end, you'll have an acrostic poem, like this one:

Munching

Ice cream

Daring

Delightful

Library

Energetic

Tigers

Oranges

Nice

Congratulations, you are a poet! Take your acrostic poem home and show it off to your family and friends. Be sure to fill out an "I Did a DIY Activity!" slip and put it in the raffle box; you might win a fabulous prize!

I Did a DIY Activity!

If you did an activity at the DIY station, please fill out this form and drop it in the raffle box. You might win a fabulous prize!

My name is _____.

I am _____ years old.

My phone number is _____.

The activity I did was:

- ❏ 24-Hour Poem
- ❏ Illustrate a Poem
- ❏ Repurposed-Book Poem
- ❏ Shape Poem
- ❏ Acrostic Poem

I Did a DIY Activity!

If you did an activity at the DIY station, please fill out this form and drop it in the raffle box. You might win a fabulous prize!

My name is _____.

I am _____ years old.

My phone number is _____.

The activity I did was:

- ❏ 24-Hour Poem
- ❏ Illustrate a Poem
- ❏ Repurposed-Book Poem
- ❏ Shape Poem
- ❏ Acrostic Poem

I Did a DIY Activity!

If you did an activity at the DIY station, please fill out this form and drop it in the raffle box. You might win a fabulous prize!

My name is _____.

I am _____ years old.

My phone number is _____.

The activity I did was:

- ❏ 24-Hour Poem
- ❏ Illustrate a Poem
- ❏ Repurposed-Book Poem
- ❏ Shape Poem
- ❏ Acrostic Poem

I Did a DIY Activity!

If you did an activity at the DIY station, please fill out this form and drop it in the raffle box. You might win a fabulous prize!

My name is _____.

I am _____ years old.

My phone number is _____.

The activity I did was:

- ❏ 24-Hour Poem
- ❏ Illustrate a Poem
- ❏ Repurposed-Book Poem
- ❏ Shape Poem
- ❏ Acrostic Poem

Books for Poetry Month

The following are books involving poetry in their plots. Other books for Poetry Month will be easy to find; visit the 808–811s for poetry, and the 921s for biographies of poets.

Creech, Sharon. *Hate That Cat.* Joanna Cotler, 2008. Upper Elementary/Teen.

    Miss Stretchberry understands why Jack hates a particular cat. She helps him to overcome the loss of his beloved dog and his hatred for the cat through poetry. Sequel to *Love That Dog* (2001).

Dotlich, Rebecca Kai. *Bella & Bean.* Atheneum, 2009. Primary.

    Bella is trying to write, but Bean won't stop distracting her! As a result, Bella's poem turns out (surprisingly) better than she had planned.

Esbaum, Jill. *Stanza.* Harcourt, 2009. Primary.

    During the day, Stanza the dog and his two trouble-making brothers terrorize the city. At night, however, Stanza writes poetry in secret.

Gutman, Dan. *Ms. Coco Is Loco!* HarperCollins, 2007. Upper Elementary.

    Poetry Month is here, and Ms. Coco is crazy for poetry. A.J., a student in Ms. Coco's class, wonders if things can possibly return to normal after Poetry Month.

Hesse, Karen. *Out of the Dust.* Scholastic, 1997. Upper Elementary/Teen.

    A series of poems reveal 15-year-old Billie Jo's hardships on an Oklahoma wheat farm during the dust bowl years of the Depression.

Kephart, Beth. *Undercover.* HarperTeen, 2007. Teen.

    Elisa, a low-profile high school sophomore with a flair for writing poetry, becomes more outgoing, thanks to her talent.

Pearson, Susan. *Slugs in Love.* Marshall Cavendish, 2006. Primary.

    Marylou and Herbie, two garden slugs, write poems in slime to one another but find meeting nearly impossible.

Scieszka, Jon and Lane Smith. *Science Verse.* Viking, 2004. Primary/Upper Elementary.

    After a teacher claims that the poetry of science can be heard in everything, a student begins hearing science verses that are based on well-known poems.

Smith, Charles. *Rimshots: Basketball, Pix, Rolls, and Rhythms.* Dutton, 1999. Upper Elementary/Teen.

    Stories and poems about basketball.

Yolen, Jane. *My Uncle Emily.* Philomel, 2009. Primary.

    Six-year-old Gilbert has unique experiences growing up next door to his aunt, the poet Emily Dickinson.

From *DIY Programming and Book Displays: How to Stretch Your Programming without Stretching Your Budget and Staff* by Amanda Moss Struckmeyer and Svetha Hetzler. Santa Barbara, CA: Libraries Unlimited. Copyright © 2010.

5

May: Museums

In May, we celebrate National Museum Month. This is the perfect time to highlight your library's art-related materials and encourage creative thinking. Children especially love to express themselves artistically, but patrons of all ages will enjoy DIY activities that call for artistic expression and knowledge of well-known art. Individuals who consider themselves unartistic will also find something of interest at this month's DIY station, where they can estimate the number of museum-themed items in a jar or match paintings with their titles. Don't limit your activities only to art, though; there are many types of museums, so be sure to incorporate themes from any local museums (historical, natural, musical, and so on).

DISPLAY IDEAS FOR MUSEUM MONTH

The theme of museums lends itself naturally to displays. Old wall calendars, art magazines, and discarded books are great resources for colorful photographs of well-known artwork. Hang these pictures on a bulletin board or around the library to highlight the DIY theme.

Local museums of all kinds are generally happy to supply brochures and other materials for display as well. This not only enhances the theme but also provides extra advertising for the museums. Local museums may even be willing to donate day passes or small souvenirs as prizes for DIY activities.

Display cases can be filled with art supplies, such as paint brushes, clay, and ribbon. Books about art (both fiction and nonfiction) are also great additions to displays this month.

EXTENSIONS ON THE THEME

Museum Night

Museum-related programs appeal to patrons of all ages and abilities. A "Museum Night" is a simple way to allow individuals to display their own artwork. Create fliers advertising this event and place them at the DIY station, and advertise as you would any other program, through your library Web site, newsletter, and other channels. Designate a one-hour time slot in the afternoon for patrons to drop off their projects. Library staff sets up the museum and hangs the art, and library guests are invited to walk through during a three-hour window of time during the evening. Snacks and classical music make this program feel even fancier! Exhibitors are welcome to pick up their projects that night or the following day.

Making Mobiles

Making mobiles is a simple, gratifying art project that requires very few materials. A coat hanger, a ball of string, and a few miscellaneous items can be combined to create a lovely mobile! Libraries focusing on the environment might offer programs for patrons to make mobiles or other projects out of trash or recyclables.

Statue, Statue

If space allows, play a game of "Statue, Statue" during story time for older preschoolers (ages 4–5). Participants will enjoy pretending to be statues in a museum or statue shop. Children move freely around the room until the leader (the librarian) gives a signal. This can be a bell, whistle, or simply the word "stop." Children freeze in place, as statues. The librarian walks around the room, asking each child what he or she is. Children respond by stating what they are pretending to be and coming to life for a few seconds. For example, a child might say, "I'm a ballerina," and then twirl around. After demonstrating, children "freeze" again. When the librarian has given each child a chance to demonstrate, the round is over; play again or move on to the next activity.

BOOKLISTS FOR MUSEUM MONTH

You'll find a reproducible booklist at the end of this chapter. Use it as a handout or a starting point for your book display or book basket. Patrons may wish to check these books out or look at them for inspiration while completing DIY activities. Find other museum-related books in your own collection to include in the display as well; cull from all sections and genres, including picture books, fiction and nonfiction, children's, teen, and adult. We have included chiefly books about museums, but books about art, architecture, natural history, and other museum-related topics would be useful in the DIY book display as well.

Activity 1 (Fill-a-Frame) also includes a brief, specific booklist of titles with illustrations of different types of frames. Library visitors may find these books useful when completing this activity. Place them in a separate basket or mark them as "Fill-a-Frame Helpers" to boost their accessibility.

Activity 1: Fill-a-Frame

Age Level: Pre-K through Teen

Activity Time: Varies widely, depending on the involvement level of the patron

What It Is: In this creative art activity, each library visitor designs a piece of artwork, names his or her masterpiece, and decorates a frame for it. The "Fill-a-Frame" activity sheets feature large spaces for artwork as well as white space for decorating the frames. Frames might be very simple or very intricate with many details; designing this will be half of the fun of completing this project! Activity sheets also include a nameplate at the bottom of the frames, where participants can write the titles of their new creations and their own names. This adds to the museum feel of the activity, since artwork in museums is usually accompanied by plates bearing title and artist information. The two different (but very similar) styles of activity sheets accommodate horizontal or vertical artwork.

How It's Done: To complete this activity, patrons help themselves to activity sheets, draw inside the frames, decorate the frames, and fill in the nameplates. Depending on staffing and space in your library, you might choose to instruct library visitors to take their finished projects home. We ask participants to turn their finished activity sheets in at the Help Desk, so that we can post them in our very own museum, which we add to continually and display all month long. This museum is located on a wall near the DIY station, so patrons can get ideas from others and see their own artwork anytime they visit. Fill-a-Frame instructions and activity sheets are included here; copy them directly or create your own!

Materials Needed

- Activity sheets
- Crayons, pencils, magic markers, or other art supplies
- Patron instructions

A Few Days Ahead

- Photocopy activity sheets.
- Generate patron instructions, or copy the instructions included in this book.

Opening Day

- Display instructions in a sign holder on the DIY table, or post them on a wall nearby.
- Place activity sheets in an easily accessed place on the table along with crayons or other art supplies.
- You may want to complete an activity sheet and display it at the DIY station as an example. A completed example is included with the reproducible patterns for this activity.

Tips and Flourishes

- Challenge participants to stretch their imaginations by limiting themselves to using just three colors (or fewer!) for this project. This works well with crayons, because a variety of shades and textures are possible. If library resources and staffing allow, pack a small plastic box of embellishments to keep at the Help Desk for visitors to borrow and

Activity 1: Fill-a-Frame (*Continued*)

incorporate into their projects. These might include glitter, stickers, fancy paper, glue, scissors, plastic gems, or other items.

- Create your own museum on a bulletin board or wall by collecting patron activity sheets and displaying them. This is a fun way for the library to highlight the DIY station and for participants to show off their work.

Booklist

Displaying books featuring illustrations of a variety of types of frames at the DIY station will help patrons find inspiration for decorating their own frames during this activity. Browse through your library's art section to find these, or try the titles listed below:

Hendry, Linda. *Making Picture Frames.* Kids Can Press, 1999.

Hodge, Steve. *Picture Frames.* Smart Apple Media, 2007.

Kistler, Vivian Carli. *The Complete Guide to Framing and Displaying Artwork.* Creative Publishing International, 2009.

Phillips, Matt. *Make Your Own Frames!* Williamson, 2001.

Rapko, Norma. *Embellished Memories: Decorating Mats and Frames.* Martingale and Company, 2008.

Rhatigan, Joe. *Decorating Frames: 45 Picture-Perfect Projects.* Lark Books, 2003.

Spencer, Joyce. *Fabulous Framing.* Sally Milner, 2000.

Reproducible patron instructions and activity sheets follow; feel free to copy or adapt them.

Fill-a-Frame Instructions

Welcome to the DIY station! Enjoy creating a piece of artwork for our museum!

1. Take an activity sheet from the stack on the table. There are two styles to choose from.

2. Draw a picture inside the frame. Your masterpiece can be a picture of anything!

3. You might have noticed that paintings in museums often have their titles and artists' names displayed with them. Write your name and the title of your picture on the nameplate (the rectangle) at the bottom of the frame. This way, everyone who sees your picture will know who the artist is and what the title of the picture is!

4. Don't forget to decorate your frame! Make it as simple or as fancy as you like. Take a look at some of the books in the DIY basket for frame ideas.

5. When you are finished, please hand your sheet in at the Help Desk. We'll add it to our museum here in the library!

From *DIY Programming and Book Displays: How to Stretch Your Programming without Stretching Your Budget and Staff* by Amanda Moss Struckmeyer and Svetha Hetzler. Santa Barbara, CA: Libraries Unlimited. Copyright © 2010.

Title: _____

Artist: _____

Fill-a-Frame

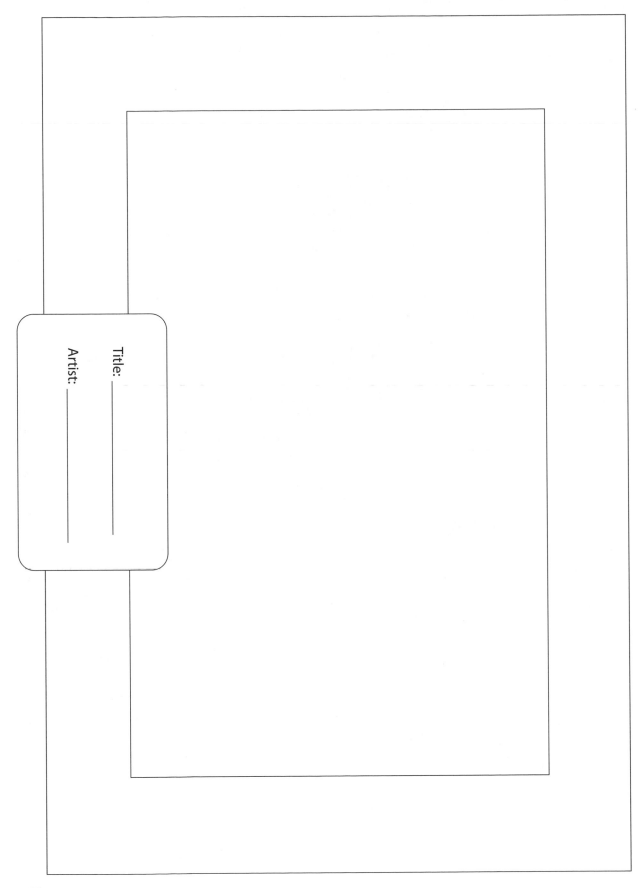

Fill-a-Frame

Title: Under The Sea

Artist: Amanda

Example of Completed Fill-a-Frame

Activity 2: Guessing Jars

Age Level: Pre-K through Teen

Activity Time: 1–5 minutes

What It Is: In this estimation activity, library guests of all ages are invited to guess the number of museum-related items in a jar.

How It's Done: Each week, a different guessing jar is placed at the DIY station. The guessing jars contain items related to the theme of museums. For example, a jar might be filled with paintbrushes, crayons, rocks or shells (if natural history museums are part of your focus), fancy buttons, miniature animals, magic markers, or other items. Place guessing slips and pencils at the DIY station. Patrons help themselves to guessing slips, fill in their guesses and contact information, and place the slips in the raffle box. The person whose guess is closest to the actual number of items in each jar wins the jar and its contents.

Materials Needed

- Guessing slips
- Pencils
- Large jars or other transparent containers (quart-size canning jars work well)
- Items to put inside the guessing jars
- Patron instructions

A Few Days Ahead

- Photocopy and cut guessing slips.
- Fill jars with items, being sure to count and record the number of items in each jar.
- Generate patron instructions, or copy the instructions included in this book.

Opening Day

- Display instructions in a sign holder on the DIY table, or post them on a wall nearby.
- Place guessing slips in an easily accessed place on the table along with pencils.
- Place one of the guessing jars at the DIY table.

As the Month Progresses

- Each week, change the guessing jar and collect the slips from the raffle box.
- Call the winners of each guessing jar. Congratulate them and invite them to come in to the library to collect their treasures!

Tips and Flourishes

- This activity is great for all ages because it is quick, engaging, and compelling. Consider adding to the appeal by photographing the winners of the guessing jars (after receiving parent/guardian permission) and displaying these photographs in the library on a special "Congratulations, Guessers!" poster, or submitting them to the local newspaper.
- If this activity is a success, consider making it a permanent part of your DIY station. Each month, different thematic items can be placed inside the jars.
- If changing the jar each week is too much, change the jar every other week, or just have one jar all month long. Another option is to have several guessing jars on display at the

Activity 2: Guessing Jars (*Continued*)

same time. For example, a paintbrush jar, a crayon jar, and a rock jar might all be displayed together for the entire month. Having guessing slips in different colors helps to minimize confusion; in addition, be sure to customize the guessing slips. For instance, the slips for the paintbrush jar might be blue and read, "How many paintbrushes are in the jar?" while the slips for the crayons might be red and read, "How many crayons are in the jar?"

Reproducible patron instructions and guessing slips follow. Two types of guessing slips are included: one general slip that could be used with any item and one that shows customized slips for jars full of different items.

Guessing Jar

Welcome to the DIY station! Can you guess how many items are in the jar?

1. Take a guessing slip from the stack on the table.

2. Fill in the slip with your name, age, and telephone number.

3. Place your slip into the raffle box.

At the end of the week, we'll read all of the guesses. The person whose guess is closest to the actual number of items will win the entire jar! We'll put a new guessing jar in the DIY station each week during May.

Have fun guessing!

How Many Items Are in the Jar?

Your name: _____

Your age: _____ Your phone number: _____

Number of items you think are in the jar: _____

How Many Items Are in the Jar?

Your name: _____

Your age: _____ Your phone number: _____

Number of items you think are in the jar: _____

How Many Items Are in the Jar?

Your name: _____

Your age: _____ Your phone number: _____

Number of items you think are in the jar: _____

How Many Items Are in the Jar?

Your name: _____

Your age: _____ Your phone number: _____

Number of items you think are in the jar: _____

How Many Crayons Are in the Jar?

Your name: _____

Your age: _____ Your phone number: _____

Number of crayons you think are in the jar: _____

How Many Crayons Are in the Jar?

Your name: _____

Your age: _____ Your phone number: _____

Number of crayons you think are in the jar: _____

How Many Crayons Are in the Jar?

Your name: _____

Your age: _____ Your phone number: _____

Number of crayons you think are in the jar: _____

Activity 3: Museum Match-Up

Age Level: Upper Elementary through Teen

Activity Time: 5–30 minutes

What It Is: In this activity, library guests match famous works of art with the museums in which the artwork is housed. "Museum Match-Up" activity sheets include two columns. The left column contains titles and artists of famous paintings, and in the right column are the names and locations of the museums where those paintings are kept. Patrons draw lines between the items in the two columns to indicate which piece of artwork matches each museum.

How It's Done: Each patron takes an activity sheet and pencil and then sets to work matching artworks and museums. Some participants might know the answers off the tops of their heads; others may need to refer to books or the Internet. We ask individuals to place their finished activity sheets in the raffle box so that we can choose a prize winner at random at the end of the month.

Materials Needed

- Activity sheets
- Pencils

A Few Days Ahead

- Photocopy activity sheets.

Opening Day

- Display activity sheets in an easily accessed place on the DIY table along with pencils.

Tips and Flourishes

- Near the DIY station, consider hanging reproductions of the artwork mentioned in this activity. Find these reproductions in wall calendars or discarded books.
- On the library Web site, include links to museum Web sites where patrons can find the correct answers to the "Museum Match-Up." Also, display reference books containing information on the artwork at or near the DIY station.
- Of course, you are welcome to vary the titles and types of artwork included in the "Museum Match-Up" activity!

A reproducible activity sheet follows; feel free to copy or adapt it.

Museum Match-Up

Match the following paintings with the museums in which they are housed. Draw lines to match each piece of artwork with the correct museum. Feel free to use library books and the Internet to help find the answers.

Works of Art	Museums
Mona Lisa by Leonardo da Vinci	Milwaukee Art Museum Milwaukee, WI
American Gothic by Grant Wood	Art Institute of Chicago Chicago, IL
Campbell's Soup by Andy Warhol	The National Gallery of Art Washington, DC
The Boating Party by Mary Cassatt	Louvre Paris, France
The Flower Carrier by Diego Rivera	San Francisco Museum of Modern Art San Francisco, CA

After completing this activity sheet, please place it in the raffle box for your chance to win this month's DIY prize.

Your name: _____ Your age: _____

Your phone number: _____

From *DIY Programming and Book Displays: How to Stretch Your Programming without Stretching Your Budget and Staff* by Amanda Moss Struckmeyer and Svetha Hetzler. Santa Barbara, CA: Libraries Unlimited. Copyright © 2010.

Activity 4: Name That Painting

Age Level: Elementary through Teen

Activity Time: 3–5 minutes

What It Is: Activity sheets include a list of titles and artists of well-known paintings. Reproductions of the paintings are displayed nearby, but each is marked with a number rather than its title and artist. Library visitors match each reproduction with the corresponding title and artist.

How It's Done: Each patron picks up an activity sheet and pencil at the DIY station and, looking at the artwork hanging nearby, writes the number of each painting next to the correct title and artist. Completed activity sheets are placed in the raffle box.

Materials Needed

- Activity sheets
- Pencils
- Reproductions of artwork (find these in wall calendars, on greeting cards, or in discarded books)

A Few Days Ahead

- Photocopy activity sheets.
- Label each artwork reproduction with a number (1–5).

Opening Day

- Place activity sheets and pencils at the DIY station.
- Hang the labeled artwork nearby.

Tips and Flourishes

- Our activity sheet contains titles of paintings we happened to have on hand from old calendars; feel free to change the artwork to suit your resources.
- Our "Name That Painting" activity is relatively simple, because the titles clearly match the subject matter. Consider creating a more challenging "Name That Painting" sheet for older library guests. Include more paintings, or include paintings that aren't easily identified by their titles. Suggest that participants use the Internet or reference books to find the answers.

   A reproducible activity sheet follows; feel free to copy or adapt it.

Name That Painting!

Take a look at the famous paintings hanging on the wall. Can you match each name with the correct painting? Write the number of the painting next to its name. When you are finished, please fill out the information about yourself and put this paper in the DIY raffle box. Have fun!

_____ *The Lacemaker* by Jan Vermeer

_____ *The Reader* by Jean-Honore Fragonard

_____ *Two Girls Reading* by Pablo Picasso

_____ *The Bookworm* by Carl Spitzweg

Hint: The bookworm is standing on a ladder!

_____ *The Library* by Jacob Lawrence

Name: _____

Age: _____

Phone number: _____

Please put your completed sheet in the raffle box for your chance to win a prize!

From *DIY Programming and Book Displays: How to Stretch Your Programming without Stretching Your Budget and Staff* by Amanda Moss Struckmeyer and Svetha Hetzler. Santa Barbara, CA: Libraries Unlimited. Copyright © 2010.

Museum Book List

Are you looking for a great book about museums? Try these! If you need help finding them, use our online catalog or ask a reference librarian.

Allison, Jennifer. *Gilda Joyce: The Dead Drop*. Dutton, 2009. Upper Elementary/Teen.

> When 14-year-old Gilda Joyce works as an intern at the International Spy Museum in Washington, D.C., over the summer, she solves an important mystery. If you like this book, try other books about Gilda Joyce!

Balliett, Blue. *The Calder Game*. Scholastic, 2008. Upper Elementary/Teen.

> Seventh-grader Calder Pillay inexplicably disappears from an English village, along with a sculpture by Alexander Calder. Friends Petra and Tommy come in from Chicago to help Calder's father find him. Look for *The Wright 3* and *Chasing Vermeer*, also in this series.

Cummings, Pat. *Harvey Moon, Museum Boy*. HarperCollins, 2008. Primary.

> Harvey takes his pet lizard, Zippy, along on a school field trip to a museum. Zippy gets loose, and a wild adventure follows.

Cussler, Clive. *The Navigator*. G. P. Putnam's Sons, 2007. Teen/Adult.

> The NUMA team is on the case of someone who killed for a statue stolen from the Baghdad Museum many years ago.

Guidone, Lisa M. *What Happens at a Museum?* Weekly Reader, 2009. Primary.

> A nonfiction book explaining what goes on at a museum.

Konigsburg, E. L. *From the Mixed-Up Files of Mrs. Basil E. Frankweiler*. Atheneum, 1967. Upper Elementary.

> Twelve-year-old Claudia and her younger brother run away and live in the Metropolitan Museum of Art, making some surprising discoveries as they do so.

Krulik, Nancy. *Katie Kazoo, Switcheroo: No Bones about It*. Grosset & Dunlap, 2004. Upper Elementary.

> While third-grader Katie is on a field trip to a natural history museum, something very strange happens to her.

Lehman, Barbara. *Museum Trip*. Houghton, 2006. Primary.

> This wordless picture book shows a boy's imaginary journey into some of the exhibits he sees during a field trip to a museum.

O'Connor, Jane. *Fancy Nancy at the Museum*. HarperCollins, 2008. Primary.

> Fancy Nancy is excited to visit the art museum with her class, but the very bus ride makes Nancy feel not-so-fancy.

Scieszka, Jon. *Seen Art?* Viking, 2005. Primary.

> A boy wanders through the Museum of Modern Art looking for his friend, Art.

From *DIY Programming and Book Displays: How to Stretch Your Programming without Stretching Your Budget and Staff* by Amanda Moss Struckmeyer and Svetha Hetzler. Santa Barbara, CA: Libraries Unlimited. Copyright © 2010.

6

June: Water

The month of June signifies the start of summer and conjures up many images. Beaches, pools, ice-cold lemonade, sprinklers, boats, and thunderstorms are summer icons, and they all share the commonality of water. June is an ideal time to explore the theme of water, providing a natural way to attract and connect library visitors with their seasonal experiences. The water-themed DIY activities this month include adopting a pirate name, sensory and estimation activities using water-related items, and communal bulletin board decorating. A reproducible booklist of water-themed books and "I Did a DIY Activity" sheets can be found at the end of this chapter.

DISPLAY IDEAS FOR WATER MONTH

Activity 2, "Create a Library Aquarium," is an interactive display that grows with each contribution. Consider mounting aquarium accessories on a bulletin board to give a three-dimensional effect to the display. Contact your local zoo, aquarium, or natural history museum for posters, pictures, or brochures for added interest and inspiration. Be sure to have a display of books about fish and other sea creatures near the bulletin board for patrons to browse and check out.

Interspersing the display of books with beach, ocean, and aquarium props such as seashells, shovels and pails, inflatable pool toys, driftwood, coral, and beach towels adds interest and depth. For added whimsy, consider displaying books in a child's plastic pool.

EXTENSIONS ON THE THEME

Water-themed programs are easy to promote during the summer months. For babies, toddlers, and preschoolers, offer beach-, bath-, or laundry-themed story times, craft programs, and play literacy activities. For early elementary school-aged children, 'tweens, and families try the following: a water-exploration program where kids and families can try simple water science experiments, a library treasure hunt or scavenger hunt, a "fishing for fiction" program where participants have a chance to show off their literary knowledge, or a paper-craft program where participants may make origami boats and treasure maps. For teens or adults, a library luau, a designer flip-flop program, a tie-dye workshop, a movie matinee, or a book-to-film discussion are appealing.

Activity 1: What's Your Pirate Name?

Age Level: Pre-K through Teen

Activity Time: 5 minutes

What It Is: This is a decoding activity that results in fun and silly results. Patrons will most likely want to decode names of their friends and family as well.

How It's Done: Patrons read the instructions and pick up a "Pirate Name Changing Chart" to transform their "regular" name into a pirate name. Participants are invited to complete an "I Did a DIY Activity" sheet using their regular and pirate names. Completed "I Did a DIY Activity" sheets are placed in the raffle box for a chance to win a prize.

Materials Needed

- Patron instruction sheet
- "Pirate Name Changing Chart"
- Pencils

A Few Days Ahead

- Generate instructions, or copy the instructions included in this book.
- Generate a "Pirate Name Changing Chart," or copy the one included in this book.

Opening Day

- Display instructions in a clear sign holder or on a wall near the DIY station.
- Place "Pirate Name Changing Charts" and pencils at the DIY station.

Tips and Flourishes

- Consider posting the names of all the pirates who have visited the DIY station. This will help patrons understand the activity and encourage participation. For example, the wall or bulletin board near your DIY station may read: "Ahoy Mateys! Check Out All the Pirates Who Have Found Treasure on Library Island." The slogan can be followed by a list of transformed "Pirate Names."
- Display a variety of pirate fiction and nonfiction books for browsing and checkout.

Booklist

Displaying books about pirates will encourage participation at the DIY station and will likely increase the circulation of library materials. Browse through the library's fantasy fiction, picture book, and nonfiction collections, or try the titles listed here:

Andreae, Giles. *Captain Flinn and the Pirate Dinosaurs: Missing Treasure!* Margaret K. McElderry Books, 2008.

Crimi, Carolyn. *Henry and the Crazed Chicken Pirates.* Candlewick Press, 2009.

DiCamillo, Kate. *Louise: The Adventures of a Chicken.* Joanna Cotler Books, 2008.

Kidd, Rob. *Pirates of the Caribbean, Jack Sparrow* series. Disney Press, 2006.

Lee, Tanith. *Piratica: Being a Daring Tale of a Singular Girl's Adventure upon the High Seas.* Dutton Children's Books, 2003.

Activity 1: What's Your Pirate Name? (*Continued*)

McDonald, Megan. *Judy Moody and Stink: The Mad, Mad, Mad, Mad Treasure Hunt.* Candlewick Press, 2009.

Rosenthal, Marc. *Archie and the Pirates.* Joanna Cotler Books, 2009.

Spangler, Brie. *Peg Leg Peke.* Alfred A. Knopf, 2008.

Steer, Dugald. *Pirateology.* Candlewick Press, 2006.

Yolen, Jane. *Sea Queens: Women Pirates around the World.* Charlesbridge, 2008.

Patron instructions and reproducible activity sheets follow; feel free to copy or adapt them.

What's Your Pirate Name?

1. Use the "Pirate Name Changing Chart" to help you convert your regular name into a thrilling and adventurous pirate name!

2. To decode your first name, take the first letter of your regular name and find the corresponding pirate first name in the first name column.

3. Do the same with your last name.

4. Everyone's pirate name begins with "Captain."

5. For example, if your name is Mary Smith, find M on the chart and go to the pirate first name column. Your pirate first name will be "Matey." Next, find S on the chart and go to the pirate last name column. Your pirate last name will be "Sparrow." Your full pirate name will be "Captain Matey Sparrow."

6. When you are done, fill out an "I Did a DIY Activity" sheet for your chance to win a prize.

Pirate Name Changing Chart

	Pirate First Name	Pirate Last Name
A	Aye-Aye	Ahoy
B	Buccaneer	Blackbeard
C	Count	Cannon
D	Dark Water	Desert
E	Excellent	Edwards
F	Fearsome	First Mate
G	Gangplank	Gold
H	Hooligan	Hook
I	Incredible	Island
J	Jolly	Jackman
K	Kidd	Kennit
L	Long	Loot
M	Matey	Maroon
N	Nautical	Nutt
O	Ocean	O'Malley
P	Peg Leg	Penzance
Q	Quince	Quicksilver
R	Ready	Redbeard
S	Scar	Sparrow
T	Trader	Treasure
U	Ultimate	Underground
V	Victorious	Vessel
W	Water	Walker
X	X Marks the Spot	eXit
Y	Yo-Ho-Ho	Yeller
Z	Zany	Zanzibar

Your pirate name: <u>Captain</u> _____   _____

From *DIY Programming and Book Displays: How to Stretch Your Programming without Stretching Your Budget and Staff* by Amanda Moss Struckmeyer and Svetha Hetzler. Santa Barbara, CA: Libraries Unlimited. Copyright © 2010.

Activity 2: Create a Library Aquarium

Age Level: Pre-K through Teen

Activity Time: 5–15 minutes

What It Is: This is an art activity that encourages drawing, coloring, and collage. It also is a community builder as each participant's contribution adds to the quantity and quality of the display.

How It's Done: Patrons draw or color a marine or aquatic animal of their choice to submit for the "Library Aquarium." Alternatively, patrons may create marine or aquatic plant life. Patrons leave their completed projects in a basket at the DIY station. Staff collects the completed activities and adds them to the wall or bulletin board near the DIY station. Patrons are invited to complete an "I Did a DIY Activity!" sheet. Completed "I Did a DIY Activity!" sheets are placed in the raffle box for a chance to win a prize.

Materials Needed

- Drawing paper
- Pencils, colored pencils, and crayons for drawing and coloring
- Raffle box
- Patron instruction sheet
- Shallow basket for collecting finished projects

A Few Days Ahead

- Identify wall space near the DIY station for the "Library Aquarium."
- Decorate the wall space or bulletin board with blue-tinted plastic wrap to make water on the walls, and hang green tissue paper from the ceiling to look like seaweed.
- Generate instructions, or copy the instructions included in this book.

Opening Day

- Display instructions in a clear sign holder or on a wall near the DIY station.
- Place paper, crayons, pencils, pens, labels, and a basket for submissions.

As the Month Progresses

- Add completed activities to the growing aquarium.

Tips and Flourishes

- Hang stuffed fish to create a three-dimensional effect.
- Display a variety of aquarium and marine life books for ideas.
- If available, hang posters from your local zoo or aquarium for added inspiration.
- Invite library visitors to bring decorative materials and props to enhance the aquarium.
- Contact the local zoo or aquarium for free passes to use as raffle prizes.

Activity 2: Create a Library Aquarium (*Continued*)

Booklist

Displaying books about marine life and aquariums will encourage participation and circulation of library materials. Browse through the library's picture book, fiction, and nonfiction collections, or try the titles listed here:

Ford, Christine. *Ocean's Child.* Golden Books, 2009.

Hiaasen, Carl. *Flush.* Alfred A. Knopf, 2005.

Jenkins, Steve. *Down Down Down: A Journey to the Bottom of the Sea.* Houghton Mifflin Harcourt, 2009.

Patterson, James. *Max: A Maximum Ride Novel.* Little, Brown & Co., 2009.

Sherry, Kevin. *I'm the Best Artist in the Ocean.* Dial Books for Young Readers, 2008.

Sierra, Judy. *Ballyhoo Bay.* Simon & Schuster Books for Young Readers, 2009.

Patron instructions and reproducible activity sheets follow; feel free to copy or adapt them.

Create a Library Aquarium

1. Take a drawing sheet.

2. Think of your favorite marine or aquarium animal or plant. If you need some ideas, browse through the library's marine and aquatic collection.

3. Using the pencils and crayons provided, draw your favorite marine animal or plant. Your drawing can be realistic or cartoon-like—it's up to you!

4. Leave your drawing in the basket, and we'll hang it up for you.

5. Fill out an "I Did a DIY Activity" sheet and place it in the raffle box for your chance to win a prize.

My Favorite Marine and Aquarium Animal or Plant

Name of marine plant or animal: _____

Activity 3: Mystery Box: It's a Wet and Watery World

Age Level: Pre-K through Upper Elementary

Activity Time: 5–10 minutes

What It Is: This is a sensory activity that challenges the participant's sense of touch. Patrons will try and decipher objects that are associated with water through tactile exploration.

How It's Done: Patrons put their hand in the "mystery box" to decide what objects are inside. After challenging their sense of touch, participants are invited to fill out a small questionnaire that serves as a raffle entry for a chance to win a prize.

Materials Needed

- Shoe box or other small box
- Scissors
- Rubber band
- Various common, small objects associated with water, such as an umbrella, a straw, a sponge, leaves, and swimming goggles. Be careful not to include sharp objects.
- Patron instruction sheet
- Patron questionnaire
- Pencils

A Few Days Ahead

- Prepare your mystery box:
  - Cut an opening at one of the small ends of a box; a shoe box is a good choice. Make sure the opening is big enough for a hand to reach inside but not so big that you can see what is inside.
  - Place the items inside the shoe box. Depending on the size of your box and objects, you may need to use a few boxes.
  - Put the lid back on the shoe box and secure the lid to the box with a rubber band.
- Generate questionnaires, or copy the questionnaire included in this chapter.
- Generate instructions, or copy the instructions included in this chapter.

Opening Day

- Display instructions in a clear sign holder or on a wall near the DIY station.
- Place the mystery box at the DIY station.
- Place questionnaires, pencils, and raffle box at the DIY station.

Tips and Flourishes

- To prevent objects from moving around inside the mystery box, you may fasten the objects with masking tape.

Activity 3: Mystery Box: It's a Wet and Watery World (*Continued*)

- To heighten your participants' excitement, you may ask your patrons to secure a blindfold around their eyes before reaching into the mystery box. By using a blindfold, patrons may achieve a greater awareness of their sense of touch.
- Consider displaying books from your nonfiction collection about the five senses.

Patron instructions and reproducible activity sheets follow; feel free to copy or adapt them.

Mystery Box: It's a Wet and Watery World

1. Secure a blindfold around your eyes, or close your eyes.

2. Reach inside the mystery box.

3. Try and identify the water-related objects. (Hint: There are five objects inside.)

4. Fill out the questionnaire with the pencil provided, and place it in the raffle box for your chance to win a prize.

Mystery Box Questionnaire

Name the five water-related objects inside the mystery box.

Place this questionnaire in the raffle box for a chance to win a prize.

1. _____
2. _____
3. _____
4. _____
5. _____

Your name: _____

Your age: _____ Your phone number: _____

Mystery Box Questionnaire

Name the five water-related objects inside the mystery box.

Place this questionnaire in the raffle box for a chance to win a prize.

1. _____
2. _____
3. _____
4. _____
5. _____

Your name: _____

Your age: _____ Your phone number: _____

Activity 4: Guess How Many Pieces of Saltwater Taffy Are in the Jar

Age Level: Pre-K through Teen

Activity Time: 5 minutes

What It Is: This is an estimation activity encouraging patrons of all ages to guess the number of pieces of saltwater taffy in a jar.

How It's Done: Patrons pick up a guessing slip and pencil from the DIY station. After taking a good look at the taffy jar, participants write down their estimations on the guessing slip and are invited to place their guesses in the raffle box for a chance to win the jar filled with saltwater taffy.

Materials Needed

- Quart-size mason jars
- Large bag of saltwater taffy
- Guessing slips
- Pencils
- Raffle box to collect guessing slips

A Few Days Ahead

- Generate or photocopy guessing slips.
- Fill the saltwater taffy jar, being sure to count and record the number of taffy pieces in the jar.

Opening Day

- Display the saltwater taffy jar, guessing slips, and pencils at the DIY station.

Tips and Flourishes

- Consider using other items associated with water, such as pebbles, small shells, straws, aquarium accessories and toys, or balloons for your guessing jars.
- Consider filling your guessing jar with a variety of water-related items in assorted sizes for more of a challenge.

Patron instructions and reproducible activity sheets follow; feel free to copy or adapt them.

How Many Pieces of Saltwater Taffy Are in the Jar?

Your name: _____

Your age: _____ Your phone number: _____

Number of saltwater taffy pieces you think are in the jar: _____

How Many Pieces of Saltwater Taffy Are in the Jar?

Your name: _____

Your age: _____ Your phone number: _____

Number of saltwater taffy pieces you think are in the jar: _____

How Many Pieces of Saltwater Taffy Are in the Jar?

Your name: _____

Your age: _____ Your phone number: _____

Number of saltwater taffy pieces you think are in the jar: _____

How Many Pieces of Saltwater Taffy Are in the Jar?

Your name: _____

Your age: _____ Your phone number: _____

Number of saltwater taffy pieces you think are in the jar: _____

I Did a DIY Water Activity!

Circle any or all of the activities you participated in, and drop this slip into the raffle box for your chance to win a prize!

What's Your Pirate Name?   Create a Library Aquarium

Mystery Box   Saltwater Taffy Guessing Jar

Your name: _____

Your pirate name (if you changed your name): _____

Your age: _____ Your phone number: _____

I Did a DIY Water Activity!

Circle any or all the activities you participated in, and drop this slip into the raffle box for your chance to win a prize!

What's Your Pirate Name?   Create a Library Aquarium

Mystery Box   Saltwater Taffy Guessing Jar

Your name: _____

Your pirate name (if you changed your name): _____

Your age: _____ Your phone number: _____

Dip, Dive, and Splash into Books about Water

Barrett, Judi. *Cloudy with a Chance of Meatballs.* Atheneum, 1978. Primary.

    The town of Chewandswallow is plagued with wacky weather where the rain, snow, and wind bring down food.

Hiaasen, Carl. *Flush.* Knopf, 2005. Upper Elementary.

    An environmental mystery set in the Florida Keys.

Hoffman, Alice. *Aquamarine.* Scholastic, 2002. Teen.

    Best friends Hailiey and Claire discover a love-struck mermaid at the bottom of a pool at the Capri Beach Club.

Holm, Jennifer. *Babymouse, Beach Babe.* Random House, 2006. Upper Elementary.

    Babymouse and her family head to the beach for a summer vacation in this graphic novel.

Junge, Sebastian. *The Perfect Storm: A True Story of Men against Sea.* Norton, 1997. Adult.

    A true account of a commercial fishing boat that is tragically caught in the center of a dangerous storm.

Kessler, Liz. *The Tail of Emily Windsnap.* Candlewick Press, 2004. Upper elementary.

    After taking swimming lesson, 12 year old Emily learns she is half-mermaid and discovers a whole new world.

Lee, Suzy. *Wave.* Chronicle Books, 2008. Primary.

    A wordless picture book depicting a little girl's day at the beach.

Riordan, Rick. *The Lightning Thief.* Hyperion, 2005. Teen.

    Percy is sent to Camp Half-Blood where he learns his father is Poseidon, god of the sea. He is soon on a quest to prevent a war between the gods.

Sheth, Kashmira. *Monsoon Afternoon.* Peachtree, 2008. Primary.

    A young boy and his grandfather discover many things they can do and see in an afternoon during India's monsoon season.

Watt, Melanie. *Scaredy Squirrel at the Beach.* Kids Can Press, 2008. Primary.

    Scaredy Squirrel is scared of everything. He very carefully plans a trip to the beach and has fun despite his fears.

7

July: Ice Cream

National Ice Cream Month is celebrated in the United States every July, and the third Sunday of July is National Ice Cream Day. Tapping into the national popularity of ice cream is a perfect way to showcase the public library as a gathering place for your community. The DIY station this month focuses on activities that grow with community participation; the results of all participants' contributions are seen as patrons attempt to build the "world's largest ice cream cone" or create a "funky flavors" menu.

You can use the ideas from this chapter to explore other popular food items such as pizza, sandwiches, donuts, or cookies throughout the year. Patrons enjoy DIY activities that fuse together culinary and literary interests, and your DIY station will provide a great opportunity to feature your library's nonfiction cookery collection, as well as your "foodie" fiction and nonfiction.

DISPLAY IDEAS FOR ICE CREAM MONTH

Who doesn't love ice cream? The activities included in this chapter serve as interactive displays as your patrons contribute to a growing ice cream cone and flavor menu. Ice cream–related products from the "Let's Go Shopping" activity help add dimension to your display, further stimulating the senses.

You may want to take it a step further and create an ice-cream-parlor atmosphere by decorating a small table near the DIY station with accessories such as sundae dishes and spoons, ice cream scoops, plastic toy ice cream cones, tall milkshake glasses, and straws. Highlighting fiction and nonfiction books about ice cream will further enhance your display.

EXTENSIONS ON THE THEME

Ice cream–inspired programs are equally fun and enjoyable for teens and preschoolers. An ice cream social is a great way to showcase the library as a gathering place and central part of the community. The program is relatively easy to pull together, and gives you a great way to include all ages. Young children and families enjoy the social experience, and older kids and teens can take turns serving. Note: Be sure to have nondairy options on hand for those with lactose intolerances.

Activity 1: Create the World's Largest Ice Cream Cone!

Age Level: Pre-K through Teen

Activity Time: 5 to 15 minutes

What It Is: This is a community-building activity in which every person (or in this case scoop!) makes a difference in creating and building something much bigger than themselves. The activity also allows patrons to explore coloring and shading techniques in creating their perfect scoop of ice cream. The ice cream scoops can be very simple or sophisticated, depending on the chosen flavor's ingredients. Consider setting a display of nonfiction and fiction books about ice cream and the dairy industry nearby.

How It's Done: To complete this activity, patrons help themselves to a white paper "scoop" and crayons or colored pencils to create a scoop of ice cream depicting their favorite flavor. Patrons leave their completed scoops in a basket at the DIY station. Staff hangs the scoops, adding them to a growing paper ice cream cone. The first few layers of the cone may have five or more scoops going across the width of the cone, with the number of scoops gradually becoming smaller as the cone reaches the ceiling. To keep the DIY activity hassle-free for staff and user-friendly for your patrons, make a cone out of brown butcher paper that starts at the floor and reaches no higher than half way up to the ceiling. A simple isosceles triangle for the ice cream cone and a semicircle for the scoop of ice cream works well.

Materials Needed

- Cutout ice cream scoops
- Brown butcher paper, four feet in width and cut into a three-foot triangle for a large cone. Butcher paper can be purchased at craft supply stores.
- Crayons or colored pencils
- HandiTAK (to easily stick scoops to and remove them from the wall)
- Small basket to hold completed scoops
- Patron Instructions

A Few Days Ahead

- Prepare ice cream cone by cutting a large triangle out of brown butcher paper. Diagonal crisscrossing lines add to the authentic "cone" look.
- Ice cream scoops—draw and cut out semicircles.
- Generate patron instructions, or copy the instructions included in this book.

Opening Day

- Display instructions in a sign holder on the DIY table.
- Place ice cream scoops in an easily accessed place on the table, along with crayons or colored pencils. If available, use clean ice cream containers, acrylic ice cream sundae cups, and other ice-cream-parlor accessories to hold supplies.

Activity 1: Create the World's Largest Ice Cream Cone! (*Continued*)

- Place a small basket for completed scoops on the DIY table.
- You may want to design the first scoop for the cone as an example.

Tips and Flourishes

- If you're concerned about young patrons disturbing the cone, consider making a slightly smaller cone and placing it a few feet off the floor so it is just out of a child's reach.
- To accommodate as many scoops as possible, place the scoops horizontally side-by-side at the base. A bit of overlapping is fine and will add dimension. Allow the cone to gradually narrow as it reaches the ceiling.
- If you prefer to have patrons add their scoops themselves, be sure to provide a steady stepstool. The scoops can be added with sticky tack, which is easy to remove.

Booklist

Displaying fiction and nonfiction books on world records and community projects will help inspire participation and may encourage participating patrons to encourage friends and neighbors to take part in this activity. Browse through your library's generalities and social issues sections, or try the titles listed below:

Clark, Sondra. *77 Creative Ways Kids Can Serve.* Wesleyan University, 2008.

Donahue, Jill. *Being Cooperative.* Picture Book Windows, 2008.

Guinness Book of World Records. Guinness World Records, 2009.

Norton, Michael. *365 Ways to Change the World: How to Make a Difference—One Day at a Time.* Free Press, 2007.

Pearsall, Shelley. *All of the Above: A Novel.* Little Brown, 2006.

Skog, Susan. *The Give Back Solution: Create a Better World with Your Time, Talents, and Travel.* Source Books, 2009.

The World's Biggest Everything. Guinness World Records, 2006.

Patron instructions follow; feel free to copy or adapt them.

I Scream, You Scream, We All Scream for Ice Cream!

Help Build the World's Tallest Ice Cream Cone!

1. Take a scoop of ice cream from the ice cream carton.

2. Use crayons to create your favorite flavor. Take a look at some of the illustrations in the books on display to help you design the perfect swirl, chip, chunk, ripple, crunch, or creaminess.

3. Leave your scoop in the basket. We'll hang it up for you.

4. We know it's tempting, but remember to take only one scoop! Be sure to tell your friends about the DIY activity so they can help build the world's largest ice cream cone. Every scoop helps!

From *DIY Programming and Book Displays: How to Stretch Your Programming without Stretching Your Budget and Staff* by Amanda Moss Struckmeyer and Svetha Hetzler. Santa Barbara, CA: Libraries Unlimited. Copyright © 2010.

Activity 2: Guess the Height of the World's Tallest Ice Cream Cone!

Age Level: Kindergarten through Teen

Activity Time: 5 minutes

What It Is: This is a mathematical activity focusing on measurement and estimation. Patrons gain an understanding of height, relative heights, and various systems of measurement.

How It's Done: To complete this activity, use the patron-made world's tallest ice cream cone (from Activity 1), or create one yourself to display near the DIY station. Near the cone, display a board or poster to illustrate the length of a foot, an inch, a meter, and a centimeter. Guessing slips ask patrons to estimate the cone's height in feet and inches, and meters and centimeters. Set out the raffle box to collect estimates. The patron whose guess is closest to the actual height wins a prize. After the contest, post the winning guess next to the cone.

Materials Needed

- Photocopied activity sheets
- Pencils
- "World's largest ice cream cone" (see Activity 1 or create your own)
- Patron instruction sheet
- Poster or board showing the length of a foot, an inch, a meter, and a centimeter

A Few Days Ahead

- Generate patron instructions, or copy the instructions included in this book.
- Photocopy activity sheets.
- If Activity 1 is not presented, prepare a paper ice cream cone to display.

Opening Day

- Display instructions on a sign holder at the DIY table.
- Place activity sheets and pencils at the DIY table.

Tips and Flourishes

- Contact your local ice cream parlor and invite them to donate a gift certificate. If a donation is not possible and resources allow, consider purchasing a gift certificate. The gift certificate may be used as a prize incentive for the winners of your "Guess the Height of the World's Largest Ice Cream Cone" contest.
- Multiple winners may be chosen. Consider having separate age categories (0–5 years, 6–11 years, and 12+). A metric system winner and a U.S. customary unit winner may also be selected.
- Display books about measurement and estimation.
- Consider making a poster illustrating various measurements. Include examples of standard heights of objects and animals, such as a crayon, a paperback book, or a school bus.

Activity 2: Guess the Height of the World's Tallest Ice Cream Cone! (*Continued*)

Booklist

Displaying books on measurement and estimation will help patrons gain an understanding of the concepts behind this DIY activity. Browse through your library's mathematics section, or try the titles listed here:

Aboff, Marcie. *If You Were an Inch or a Centimeter.* Picture Window Books, 2009.

Cleary, Brian. *How Long or How Wide: A Measuring Guide.* Millbrook Press, 2007.

Goldstone, Bruce. *Great Estimations.* Henry Holt, 2006.

Mitsumasa, Anno. *Anno's Math Games.* Philomel Books, 1987.

Salzmann, Mary. *What in the World Is a Foot?* ABDO, 2009.

Sargent, Brian. *Can You Guess?* Children's Press, 2004.

Schwartz, David. *Millions to Measure.* Harper Collins, 2003.

Patron instructions and reproducible activity sheets follow; feel free to copy or adapt them.

I Scream, You Scream, We All Scream for Ice Cream!

Guess the Height of the World's Tallest Ice Cream Cone!

1. Look at the world's tallest ice cream cone, and estimate its height.

2. Use a pencil to fill out a guessing sheet.

3. The actual height of our ice cream cone will be posted at the end of the week.

Guess the Height of the World's Tallest Ice Cream Cone!

Height in feet and inches: _____

Height in meters and centimeters: _____

Your name: _____

Your age: _____ Your phone number: _____

Number of crayons you think are in the jar: _____

Guess the Height of the World's Tallest Ice Cream Cone!

Height in feet and inches: _____

Height in meters and centimeters: _____

Your name: _____

Your age: _____ Your phone number: _____

Number of crayons you think are in the jar: _____

Guess the Height of the World's Tallest Ice Cream Cone!

Height in feet and inches: _____

Height in meters and centimeters: _____

Your name: _____

Your age: _____ Your phone number: _____

Number of crayons you think are in the jar: _____

Activity 3: Funky Flavors Ice Cream Menu

Age Level: Pre-K through Teen

Activity Time: 5 to 15 minutes

What It Is: This creative writing activity allows patrons to have fun with poetic wordplay to create a bizarre and unique ice cream menu. Similar to the library ice cream cone (Activity 1), this activity is also a community builder as each patron helps contribute to the outrageous and growing menu.

How It's Done: To complete this activity, patrons help themselves to a "Funky Flavors" idea sheet and pencil and write down a unique flavor. Patrons submit their idea by placing their sheets in the flavor suggestion or raffle box. Staff collects completed idea sheets from the box and writes the flavors on the growing menu posted on the wall.

Materials Needed

- Patron instruction sheet
- Photocopied sheets of "Funky Flavors" idea slips
- Black poster board (3' × 2') taped to the wall to resemble a menu board
- Pastels, gel pens, or colored chalk for writing on the menu
- Pencils
- Flavor suggestion box

A Few Days Ahead

- Generate patron instructions, or copy the instructions included in this book.
- Photocopy "Funky Flavors" idea sheets.
- Hang black poster board on a bulletin board or a wall near the DIY station.

Opening Day

- Display instructions in a sign holder on the DIY table.
- Place "Funky Flavors" idea sheets in an easily accessed place on the table along with pencils. Consider using ice cream containers to hold idea sheets and pencils.
- Set out flavor suggestion box, which may double as a raffle entry box.

Tips and Flourishes

- Consider allowing your 'tween and teen patrons to write their flavor ideas directly onto the black poster board. Provide gel pens, colored chalk, or pastels to help replicate an authentic ice-cream-parlor menu board.
- Empty the suggestion box daily so that flavor ideas can be displayed quickly. Patrons will look forward to seeing their flavors on the menu.
- Consider featuring a special flavor of the day as inspiration.
- Hold a raffle as an incentive to participate. The "Funky Flavor" idea sheets can double as raffle slips. Your prize might be a free scoop of ice cream from a local ice cream parlor, an ice cream book, or any ice cream–related product.
- Host an ice cream story time or a play literacy ice-cream-parlor program for young patrons.

- Host a "Shakes and Smoothies" program for your 'tweens and teens. Provide blenders, ingredients, and recipes for guests to create a variety of shakes and smoothies to sample.
- Display poetry anthologies that contain poems about ice cream. Shel Silverstein's "Eighteen Flavors" from *Where the Sidewalk Ends: The Poems and Drawings of Shel Silverstein* and Jack Prelutsky's "Bleezer's Ice Cream" from *The New Kid on the Block: Poems* are likely to spark many flavorful ideas.

Patron instructions and reproducible patterns follow; feel free to copy or adapt them.

Funky Flavors Ice Cream Menu

Welcome to the DIY station! We've all heard of "31 Flavors." Can our library come up with even more? It sounds easy, but there's a catch: The flavors must be unusual, bizarre, and unique! Follow the instructions below to add your flavor idea to the Funky Flavors Menu.

1. Take a Funky Flavors idea sheet from the table.

2. Think of the funkiest ice cream flavor you can and write it down on the idea sheet. Remember, nothing is too weird!

3. Drop your idea into the flavor suggestion box.

4. Look for your suggested flavor on the menu board the next time you come to the library.

5. Fill out an "I Did a DIY Activity" slip and enter it in the raffle box for a chance to win a fabulous prize!

From *DIY Programming and Book Displays: How to Stretch Your Programming without Stretching Your Budget and Staff* by Amanda Moss Struckmeyer and Svetha Hetzler. Santa Barbara, CA: Libraries Unlimited. Copyright © 2010.

Funky Flavors

Flavor idea: _____

Your name: _____

Your age: _____ Your phone number: _____

Funky Flavors

Flavor idea: _____

Your name: _____

Your age: _____ Your phone number: _____

Funky Flavors

Flavor idea: _____

Your name: _____

Your age: _____ Your phone number: _____

Funky Flavors

Flavor idea: _____

Your name: _____

Your age: _____ Your phone number: _____

Activity 4: Let's Go Shopping for Ice Cream

Age Level: Pre-K through Teen

Activity Time: 15 minutes

What It Is: This estimation activity encourages patrons of all ages to guess the price of ice cream and ice cream–related toppings and accessories. This activity is great for all ages because it is quick and eye-catching.

How It's Done: To complete this activity, patrons help themselves to guessing slips (price tags) and pencils. Ice cream–related items such as sprinkles, sauces, marshmallows, cherries, straws, spoons, bowls, cones, empty containers of ice cream and whipped cream, gummy bears, chocolate chips, and cookies are displayed. Alternatively, a poster with photos of each product may be displayed. Patrons guess the price of one or more items. Guesses are submitted to the raffle box. At the conclusion of this DIY activity, each ice cream–related item is given as a prize to the patron whose guess is closest to the actual price.

Materials Needed

- Guessing slips (price tags)
- Pencils
- Ice cream–related products
- Patron instruction sheet

A Few Days Ahead

- Photocopy and cut guessing slips.
- Photocopy patron instruction sheet.
- Create a "This Week's Specials" poster with photos of the products to be priced.

Opening Day

- Display instructions in a sign holder on the DIY table, or post them on a wall nearby.
- Place price tags in an easily accessed place on the table along with pencils and the raffle box.
- Cover or cross out any price information on the items.
- Place ice cream–related products in a shopping basket at the DIY table.

Tips and Flourishes

- Consider placing guessing slips and pencils in a metal cash box or toy cash register to help create the feel of a market.
- Keep a receipt with the prices of the ice cream products to be priced; your participants may want to see it after winners are announced.
- Instead of displaying actual food items at your DIY station, consider placing empty containers or toy versions of these items in the shopping basket. Alternatively, you may create a poster with photos of "This Week's Specials." The poster will contain photos of the "Let's Go Shopping for Ice Cream" items to be priced.
- Consider placing circulars from local grocery stores at the DIY station to help with pricing estimations.

- Host a supermarket play literacy program for younger patrons. Read a book or two about shopping to introduce the play literacy theme. Set the program area up like a grocery store with toy food items, empty containers and packages of food items, shopping baskets, bags, toy cash registers, and play money. Encourage children to take turns acting as customers and as supermarket employees. Once your program room is set up, simply sit back and watch your young patrons' creativity bloom.

- Host an evening family "Let's Go Shopping" program. Use items from the DIY station and additional ice cream–related products not featured at the DIY station. Create interactive game show–style activities. Patrons of all ages enjoy guessing the prices of various items. Winners can take home the displayed merchandise.

- Contact the local supermarket for donations to help sponsor this DIY activity and any extended events.

- Extend the "Let's Go Shopping" DIY to other merchandise such as clothing, school supplies, or toys; anything fun, recognizable, or seasonal will attract patrons to this program.

Booklist

Displaying books about money and shopping ties in with your pricing activity and may inspire patrons to learn more about economics and product supply and demand. There are also many fiction picture books and chapter books about shopping. Browse through your library's economics section, or try the titles listed below:

10,001 Ways to Live Large on a Small Budget. Skyhorse, 2009.

Krull, Kathleen. *Supermarket.* Holiday House, 2001.

Marrewa, Jennifer. *Using Money on a Shopping Trip.* Weekly Reader Books, 2008.

Minden, Cecilia. *Smart Shopping.* Cherry Lake, 2008.

Ostyn, Mary. *Family Feasts for $75 a Week.* Oxmoor House, 2009.

Roy, Jennifer Rozines. *Money at the Store.* Marshall Cavendish Benchmark, 2007.

Reproducible patron instructions and guessing slips are found on the following pages; feel free to copy or adapt them.

Let's Go Shopping for Ice Cream!

Welcome to the DIY station! Can you guess how much the following items cost at your local supermarket?

1. Take a price tag from the cash box on the table.

2. Fill in the slip with your name, age, telephone number, the name of the item you are guessing on, and your guess at the item's price.

3. Place your slip into the raffle box.

At the end of the week, we'll read all of the price estimations. Participants with the closest guesses will win the item!

Have fun guessing!

Let's Go Shopping for Ice Cream Price Tag

Item: _____ $_____._____

Your name: _____

Your age: _____ Your phone number: _____

Let's Go Shopping for Ice Cream Price Tag

Item: _____ $_____._____

Your name: _____

Your age: _____ Your phone number: _____

Let's Go Shopping for Ice Cream Price Tag

Item: _____ $_____._____

Your name: _____

Your age: _____ Your phone number: _____

Let's Go Shopping for Ice Cream Price Tag

Item: _____ $_____._____

Your name: _____

Your age: _____ Your phone number: _____

Ice Cream Books: Read the Entire "Scoop"!

Alborough, Jez. *Ice Cream Bear.* Candlewick, 1997. Primary.
  Bear falls asleep under a broken window pane and dreams it is snowing ice cream.

Cirrone, Dorian. *The Big Scoop.* Marshall Cavendish, 2006. Upper Elementary.
  Fourth-grader Lindy Blues works to solve the mystery of the ice cream store that disappears and reappears daily.

Docherty, James. *The Ice Cream Con.* Chicken House, 2008. Teen.
  Set in Scotland, this is the story of 13-year-old Jake, who with the help of an ice cream truck comes up with a plan to outsmart the criminals in his neighborhood.

Gibbons, Gail. *Ice Cream: The Full Scoop.* Holiday House, 2006. Primary.
  A detailed history of the production and history of ice cream.

Henkes, Kevin. *Wemberly's Ice Cream Star.* Harper Festival, 2003. Primary.
  Wemberly is worried again, this time about her ice cream bar melting and dripping onto her new dress.

Keene, Carolyn. *Scream for Ice Cream.* (Nancy Drew and the Clue Crew Series). Aladdin Paperbacks, 2006. Upper Elementary.
  Nancy investigates the case of a stolen ice cream recipe.

Murdock, Catherine. *Dairy Queen.* Houghton Mifflin, 2006. Teen.
  After spending the summer running her family's dairy farm, D.J. decides to try out for her rival school's football team.

Murphy, Stuart. *Sundae Scoop.* Harper Collins, 2003. Primary.
  Using mathematical concepts, James and his friends make a variety of ice cream sundaes.

Pinkwater, Daniel. *Ice Cream Larry.* Marshall Cavendish, 1999. Primary.
  Larry the Polar Bear becomes the "spokesbear" for the Icebery Ice Cream Company.

Ried, Adam. *Thoroughly Modern Milkshakes.* W. W. Norton, 2009. Adult.
  A collection of 100 classic and contemporary milkshake recipes.

Warner, Gertrude. *The Chocolate Sundae Mystery.* (Boxcar Children Series). Albert Whitman, 1995. Upper Elementary.
  The Boxcar Children begin an investigation when ice cream and other items disappear from Mr. Brown's ice cream parlor.

From *DIY Programming and Book Displays: How to Stretch Your Programming without Stretching Your Budget and Staff* by Amanda Moss Struckmeyer and Svetha Hetzler. Santa Barbara, CA: Libraries Unlimited. Copyright © 2010.

8

August: Sports

August is a great time to celebrate sports. Students are looking forward to the start of fall sports, and in most places, the weather lends itself to being outdoors for athletic events and practices. Of course, a sports theme works any time of year. Tie this topic in with local, state, and national sporting events or the summer or winter Olympics. Highlighting sports at the DIY station engages all kinds of readers (sports enthusiasts and otherwise); watch your library's sports books jump in popularity after these programs.

DISPLAY IDEAS FOR SPORTS MONTH

Gather up lots of sports equipment for your displays this month. Footballs, baseball gloves, running shoes, swimming goggles, pom-poms, golf tees, and other athletic gear look great in a display case.

Ask library staff and well-known community members for photos of themselves playing sports. You could also invite library visitors to submit pictures of themselves playing sports or in sports uniforms to add to a display or bulletin board.

Use sports phrases, such as "Batter Up!" "Nothin' But Net!" "Touchdown!" and "Go for the Goal!" as headings on bulletin boards and other displays. Discarded books and sports magazines are good sources for pictures to include in your displays as well.

EXTENSIONS ON THE THEME

Sports Events at the Library

What better way to celebrate the sports theme than with actual athletics? Host a noncompetitive match of some type. For example, a staff versus patrons soccer game is fun and a good way to get to know library visitors.

Silly Sports

Host a "silly sports" program including a three-legged race, a leapfrog competition, a backwards-walking relay, and other goofy activities. Prizes can be just as silly as the sports are: a jar of pickles, a package of shoelaces, or a string of paper clips.

Wii Sports

If resources allow, host a Wii games workshop at the library. Have sports games available (popular Wii sports include bowling, tennis, and golf). At our library, a drop-in, all-ages format has worked well; we have the Wii system set up for a two-hour block in the program room, and anyone is welcome to drop in and play.

BOOKLISTS FOR SPORTS MONTH

You'll find a reproducible booklist at the end of this chapter. Use it as a patron handout or a starting point for your book display or book basket. Patrons may wish to check these books out or look at them for inspiration while completing DIY activities. Find other sports-related books in your own collection to include in the display as well; cull from all sections and genres, including picture books, fiction and nonfiction, children's, teen, and adult.

Activity 1: Vote for Your Favorite Sport

Age Level: Pre-K through Teen

Activity Time: 1–3 minutes

What It Is: This is a voting activity in which library guests are invited to indicate their favorite sports.

How It's Done: At the DIY station, each patron picks up a ballot and pencil, then votes for his or her favorite sport and leaves the ballot in the raffle box. Library staff collects the ballots and tabulates and posts the results.

Materials Needed

- Ballots
- Pencils
- Patron instructions

A Few Days Ahead

- Photocopy ballots.
- Generate patron instructions, or copy the instructions included in this book.

Opening Day

- Display instructions in a sign holder on the DIY table, or post them on a wall nearby.
- Place ballots in an easily accessed place on the table along with pencils.

Tips and Flourishes

- Rather than just tabulating and posting the ballot results at the end of the month, do this every week for a running tally. Library visitors will enjoy seeing which sport is in the lead at different points during the month.
- To expand this activity, create ballots with a space for an additional question, such as "Why do you like this sport?" or "Have you ever tried this sport?"

Reproducible instructions and ballots follow; feel free to copy or adapt them.

Vote for Your Favorite Sport

Let's find out what the library's favorite sport is!

You'll find ballots and pencils at the DIY station. Put your completed ballot in the raffle box.

Be sure to include your name and phone number; you could win a fabulous prize!

Check back at the DIY station at the end of the month to find out which sport got the most votes!

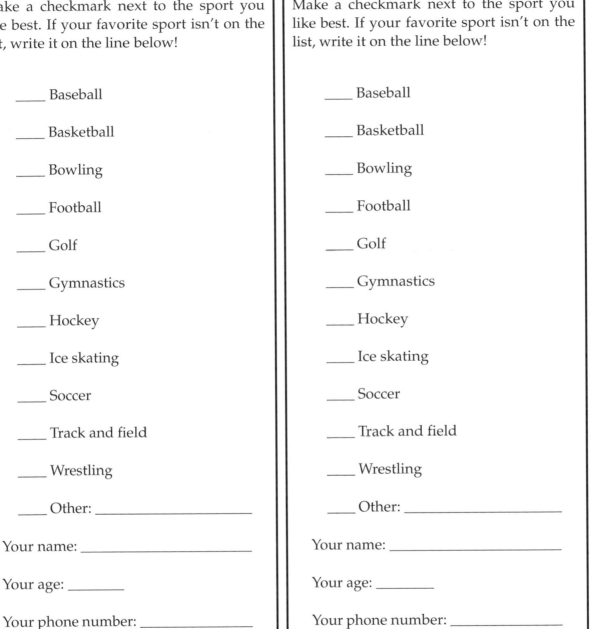

Vote for Your Favorite Sport!

Make a checkmark next to the sport you like best. If your favorite sport isn't on the list, write it on the line below!

_____ Baseball

_____ Basketball

_____ Bowling

_____ Football

_____ Golf

_____ Gymnastics

_____ Hockey

_____ Ice skating

_____ Soccer

_____ Track and field

_____ Wrestling

_____ Other: _____

Your name: _____

Your age: _____

Your phone number: _____

Vote for Your Favorite Sport!

Make a checkmark next to the sport you like best. If your favorite sport isn't on the list, write it on the line below!

_____ Baseball

_____ Basketball

_____ Bowling

_____ Football

_____ Golf

_____ Gymnastics

_____ Hockey

_____ Ice skating

_____ Soccer

_____ Track and field

_____ Wrestling

_____ Other: _____

Your name: _____

Your age: _____

Your phone number: _____

Activity 2: Design a Sports Jersey

Age Level: Pre-K through Teen

Activity Time: 5–10 minutes

What It Is: This is a creative art activity in which library visitors design original jerseys.

How It's Done: Patrons pick up activity sheets and art supplies at the DIY station and follow the instructions to design sports jerseys. Completed projects are placed in the raffle box. Library staff posts the jerseys on a wall or bulletin board near the DIY station. Because instructions are included in activity sheets, no separate instruction sheet is necessary.

Materials Needed

- Activity sheets
- Pencils
- Art supplies, such as crayons and markers

A Few Days Ahead

- Photocopy activity sheets.
- Complete an activity sheet or two to hang up as examples.

Opening Day

- Place activity sheets in an easily accessed place on the table along with pencils and art supplies.

As the Month Progresses

- Collect completed activity sheets from the raffle box. Cut off the portion containing personal information and retain it for the end-of-the-month drawing. Display the remaining part of the activity sheets on a poster or bulletin board near the DIY station.

Tips and Flourishes

- If time, space, and resources allow, make additional art supplies available. Scraps of fabric, sequins, glitter, rubber stamps, patterned paper, glue, and scissors will encourage creativity.
- Take a digital picture of each jersey and create an online photo gallery or slideshow on your library's Web site.

A reproducible activity sheet follows; feel free to copy or adapt it.

Design a Jersey

What would your ultimate sports jersey look like? Show us here! Use the art supplies at the DIY station. Put your completed sheet in the raffle box; we'll display your jersey, and you could win a fabulous prize!

What sport is your jersey for? _____

Which team (real or imagined) is your jersey for? _____

_____

Your name: _____

Your age: _____ Your phone number: _____

Activity 3: Find a Sport

Age Level: Elementary through Teen

Activity Time: 5–10 minutes

What It Is: This is a scavenger hunt–style activity in which library guests find sports books in the stacks.

How It's Done: Participants pick up activity sheets and pencils at the DIY station. Following the instructions on the activity sheets, patrons search the stacks for sports books and record their call numbers. Completed activity sheets are left in the raffle box. Because instructions are included in activity sheets, no separate instruction sheet is necessary.

Materials Needed

- Activity sheets
- Pencils

A Few Days Ahead

- Photocopy activity sheets.

Opening Day

- Display activity sheets in an easily accessed place on the DIY table along with pencils.

Tips and Flourishes

- While the activity sheet provided here leads readers to nonfiction sports books, try creating a more complex task by adding fiction books and a variety of nonfiction (biographies of sports figures, for example) to the goals in this activity.

   A reproducible activity sheet follows; feel free to copy or adapt it.

Find a Sport

There are lots of books about sports in the library! Try this scavenger hunt to find some of them.

Here are some hints for you to follow:

- Find the nonfiction section. This is where factual books are.
- Nonfiction books are organized by the numbers on their spine labels. This number is known as the **call number**.
- Our cookbooks have the call number **641**. The call numbers for sports books are higher than the call number for cookbooks.
- Our poetry books have the call number **811**. The call numbers for sports books are lower than the call number for poetry books.

When you find a sports book, fill in the following information:

I found a sports book! The title is _____ and
    the author is _____. It has _____ pages.
    This book's call number is _____.

Your name: _____

Your age: _____ Your phone number: _____

Please leave this form in the raffle box at the DIY station; you could win a fabulous prize!

From *DIY Programming and Book Displays: How to Stretch Your Programming without Stretching Your Budget and Staff* by Amanda Moss Struckmeyer and Svetha Hetzler. Santa Barbara, CA: Libraries Unlimited. Copyright © 2010.

Activity 4: Sports Match-Up

Age Level: Early Elementary through Upper Elementary

Activity Time: 3–5 minutes

What It Is: The activity sheet contains a list of book titles and a list of sports. Patrons match each title with the sport that is featured in that particular book.

How It's Done: Participants pick up activity sheets and pencils at the DIY station. Using their own knowledge of the books on the list, the catalog, or the books themselves, patrons match the book titles with the corresponding sports. Because instructions are included in activity sheets, no separate instruction sheet is necessary.

Materials Needed

- Activity sheets
- Pencils

A Few Days Ahead

- Photocopy activity sheets.

Opening Day

- Place activity sheets and pencils at the DIY station.
- Set books on display nearby (optional).

Tips and Flourishes

- Our activity sheet features picture books and early chapter books that will be accessible to elementary school-aged children. Make a sheet for teens or adults using more sophisticated titles.
- At our library, we draw a winner at random from all of the entries (not just the correct entries). We focus on participation rather than on correct answers.
- Photocopy these activity sheets onto a different color of paper from the "Find a Sport" sheets. This will make collection, tallying, and prize drawing easier.
- If resources allow, place display-only copies of the books on the list in the DIY book basket.

A reproducible activity sheet follows; feel free to copy or adapt it.

Sports Match-Up

Each of the books on this list is about a sport. Can you figure out which sport matches each book? The library catalog and the books on display will help you.

Match each book with a sport by writing the letter of the sport on the line next to the book's title.

___ *Mighty Casey* by James Preller

___ *Goalkeeper Goof* by Cari Meister

___ *D.W. Flips!* by Marc Brown

___ *Coach Hyatt Is a Riot!* by Dan Gutman

___ *Casey and Derek on the Ice* by Marty Sederman

___ *Hoop Doctor* by Jake Maddox

a. Soccer

b. Basketball

c. Hockey

d. Gymnastics

e. Football

f. Baseball

My name is _____. I am _____ years old.

My phone number is _____.

Please put this sheet in the raffle box; you could win a fabulous prize!

Sports Book List

Are you looking for a great book about sports? Try these! Also check out the **796** nonfiction section, where you'll find lots of great informational books about your favorite sports. If you need help finding books, use our online catalog or ask a reference librarian.

Adler, David. *Cam Jansen and the Sports Day Mysteries: A Super Special.* Puffin, 2009. Primary.

During Sports and Good Nutrition Day at school, super sleuth Cam Jansen solves three mysteries. If you like this book, try others about Cam Jansen!

Barber, Tiki. *Wild Card.* Simon & Schuster, 2009. Upper Elementary.

Ronde's coach has said that football is a mental game, and Ronde learns that this is true during a particularly challenging season.

Christopher, Matt. *Power Pitcher.* Little, Brown, 2008. Upper Elementary.

The first thing Jimmie does after being elected captain of his baseball team is to make himself the team's pitcher, even though the team already has a good pitcher. Jimmie's team wants their old pitcher back. Will Jimmie be able to make things right again with the team? If you like this book, look for other fast-paced sports books by Matt Christopher!

Coy, John. *Box Out.* Scholastic, 2008. Teen.

Liam, a sophomore in high school, has just made the varsity basketball team. He puts his new status on the line by taking a stand against his coach, who is insisting on participation in pregame prayers.

Feinstein, John. *Change-Up: Mystery at the World Series.* Knopf, 2009. Teen.

Stevie and Susan Carol are teenage sports writers covering the World Series. The two writers investigate a suspicious rookie pitcher.

Gleitzman, Morris. *Toad Rage.* Random House, 2004. Upper Elementary/Teen.

Limpy, a toad, leaves his swamp and sets out for the Summer Olympics in Sydney, Australia, hoping to find out why humans hate toads and to improve relations between toads and humans.

Goldish, Meish. *Michael Phelps: Anything Is Possible!* Bearport, 2009. Primary.

An introductory biography of Olympic swimmer Michael Phelps.

Hicks, Betty. *Swimming with Sharks.* Roaring Brook Press, 2008. Upper Elementary.

Rita is working hard at improving her flip turns. She's torn between remaining on the Dolphins team, where she is the best swimmer, or trying to join the Sharks with her friends, where she would likely be the worst swimmer. If you like this book, look for other books in the Gym Shorts series!

Klein, Abby. *Ready, Set, Snow!* Blue Sky Press, 2009. Primary.

The first grade has a Winter Olympics contest, and Freddy helps his class to win and show good sportsmanship at the same time.

Sports Book List (*Continued*)

Lupica, Mike. *The Million Dollar Throw.* Philomel, 2009. Upper Elementary/Teen.

Nate Brodie is a star quarterback whose family is dealing with financial problems. Nate's best friend, Abby, is going blind. When he has the opportunity to win one million dollars for completing a pass during halftime at a New England Patriot's game, Nate is overwhelmed. . . . Can he do it? Mike Lupica has written lots of other great sports books.

9

September: Extra! Extra!

This month, we feature newspapers at the DIY station. This is a great opportunity to highlight the different parts of a newspaper, as well as the selection of newspapers the library stocks. Today, many people get their news on television or online, so newspapers are not as widely read as they once were. You may be surprised at how unfamiliar young people are with newspapers. This month's DIY activities introduce participants to several parts of the newspaper. Becoming engaged in classified ads, advice columns, and headlines may pique patrons' interest; don't be surprised if, before long, your library's newspapers begin flying off the racks!

DISPLAY IDEAS FOR NEWSPAPER MONTH

Create an eye-catching display using discarded newspapers. Tack sheets of the paper up as a background for a bulletin board. Cut bold paper letters in a bright color to spell a heading for your bulletin board, such as "Extra! Extra!" or "In the News." Use the bulletin board to display completed DIY projects, fliers advertising upcoming events at the library, or other items of note.

In a display case, place a whole newspaper and an old-fashioned newsboy cap. Cut comic strips from a discarded newspaper, glue them onto colorful cardstock, and prop them up in the display case. Take pictures of library staff members reading the newspaper, and add these to the case as well.

Because patrons may wish to take their finished projects home or leave them to add to the display, a separate sheet for entering the prize drawing is practical. A reproducible page of "I Did a DIY Activity!" slips is included in this chapter.

EXTENSIONS ON THE THEME

Papier-Mâché Party

A popular use for old newspapers is making papier-mâché projects. Hold a program in which participants create sculptures with newspaper and papier-mâché paste. The paste can be made inexpensively using flour and water. Mix approximately 1 part flour to 2 parts water, aiming for a gluey consistency. Cut 1" strips of newspaper, wet them in the paste, and layer to create a unique sculpture. Balloons, toilet paper tubes, and empty tissue boxes are helpful armatures.

Picture This

Challenge patrons to take pictures of themselves reading newspapers in unique locations. These might include the beach, a restaurant, an airplane, or a shopping mall. Patrons who drop off photographs are entered in a special prize drawing, and their pictures are added to a display case or bulletin board.

Headline Mashup

Host a silly program with very little preparation and little or no cost. Cut individual words from the headlines of a discarded newspaper, and glue them to small pieces of construction paper. Place words face down on a table, and invite each person to choose three or four. Working individually or in pairs, participants create new headlines using the words they selected. Each person takes a turn telling his or her headline and a brief summary of an imaginary corresponding news article.

BOOKLIST FOR NEWSPAPER MONTH

You'll find a reproducible booklist at the end of this chapter. Use it as a patron handout or a starting point for your book display or book basket. Patrons may wish to check these books out or look at them for inspiration while completing DIY activities. Find other newspaper-related books in your own collection to include in the display as well; cull from all sections and genres, including picture books, fiction and nonfiction, children's, teen, and adult.

Activity 1: The Classifieds

Age Level: Upper Elementary through Teen

Activity Time: 5–15 minutes

What It Is: This descriptive writing activity gives patrons the chance to recommend favorite books to other readers through original classified advertisements.

How It's Done: At the DIY station, library visitors pick up activity sheets and pencils. Following the instructions posted at the DIY station, each participant writes a classified advertisement for a book of his or her choosing. Completed activity sheets are placed in the raffle box and posted by library staff. Patrons fill out "I Did a DIY Activity!" sheets for entry into this month's prize drawing.

Materials Needed

- Activity sheets
- Patron instructions
- Pencils
- Examples of classified advertisements from a real newspaper, laminated or mounted on cardstock

A Few Days Ahead

- Photocopy activity sheets.
- Generate patron instructions, or use the ones included in this book.
- Cut examples of classified advertisements from a newspaper; laminate them or mount them on cardstock.

Opening Day

- Display instructions in a sign holder on the DIY table, or post them on a wall nearby.
- Place activity sheets and examples of classified advertisements in an easily accessed place on the table along with pencils.
- You may want to complete an activity sheet and display it at the DIY station as an example.

Tips and Flourishes

- At the end of the month, compile all of the classified ads that were written into a book or binder for browsing or checkout.
- Create a display of the books written about by patrons in this activity. Laminate the activity sheets, and place each one in or near the corresponding book. Browsers might be encouraged to check a certain book out after reading another reader's advertisement!

Reproducible patron instructions and an activity sheet follow; feel free to copy or adapt them.

The Classifieds

People who have things to sell often put classified advertisements in the newspaper. Do you have something to sell? Yes, you do! Think of a favorite book that you'd like to "sell" to other people! Create a classified advertisement for the book.

Take a look at the classified advertisement examples from the real newspaper posted at the DIY station. Use these tips to help you write your own:

- Think of a catchy phrase or sentence to start out your classified advertisement. Try something like:

  Do you like books about mummies? Then this might be the book for you!

  Looking for a romantic book to read on the beach?

  Caution: This cookbook contains many tempting recipes!

- Include some basic information about the book. For example, indicate what type of book it is (romance, mystery, nonfiction, etc.). Make sure to include the book's title and the author's name.

- Explain why you like this book. For example, do you like it because it has interesting characters, a lot of magic, or great pictures?

Write your classified advertisement on an activity sheet (found at the DIY station). When you're finished, leave it in the raffle box; we'll put it on display for others to read. Be sure to fill in an "I Did a DIY Activity!" slip and put it in the raffle box. You could win a fabulous prize!

The Classifieds

Write a classified advertisement for your favorite book on the lines below. Be sure to put your finished classified ad and an "I Did a DIY Activity!" slip in the raffle box.

Book's title: _____

Book's author: _____

_____

_____

_____

_____

_____

_____

_____

_____

_____

_____

_____

Activity 2: Headliners

Age Level: Elementary through Teen

Activity Time: 1–5 minutes

What It Is: This is a brief writing activity in which library visitors create headlines.

How It's Done: Participants simply write attention-grabbing headlines. Library staff adds these to a poster or bulletin board. Patrons are also invited to fill out "I Did a DIY Activity!" slips.

Materials Needed

- Plain pieces of blank paper, cut into thirds lengthwise (this is what the headlines are written on)
- Patron instructions
- Pencils
- Examples of eye-catching headlines from real newspapers, laminated or mounted on cardstock

A Few Days Ahead

- Generate patron instructions, or copy the ones included in this book.
- Cut blank pieces of paper into thirds lengthwise.
- Cut out and laminate or mount interesting headlines from real newspapers.

Opening Day

- Display actual headlines and instructions at or near the DIY station.
- Place paper strips in an easily accessed place on the table along with pencils.

As the Month Progresses

- Library staff collects completed headlines from the raffle box and posts them near the DIY station as part of a poster or bulletin board.

Tips and Flourishes

- If time and resources allow, extend this activity by providing news articles (real or fabricated) for library guests to write headlines for. Another option is to have patrons write short articles to correspond with the headlines they create.

Reproducible patron instructions follow; feel free to copy or adapt them.

Headliners

In the newspaper, headlines grab our attention and make us interested in reading articles. This is your chance to write an attention-grabbing headline!

Think of an article you would like to read. It doesn't have to be a real article. For example, you might like to read an article about:

- New books at the library
- A cow with pink spots that scientists have discovered
- An alien visiting from outer space

Using a strip of paper from the DIY station, write a short, interesting headline that would get other people interested in reading the article. Check out some of the real headlines on our poster for inspiration.

When you're finished, put your headline in the raffle box. We'll post it as part of our display. Also, be sure to fill out an "I Did a DIY Activity!" slip and put it in the raffle box for your chance to win a fabulous prize!

Activity 3: Picture This!

Age Level: Pre-K through Teen

Activity Time: 5–10 minutes

What It Is: This is a creative art activity in which participants draw an illustration to correspond with a news article.

How It's Done: Visitors to the DIY station are provided with activity sheets and crayons. Each sheet includes a fabricated news article and space for an illustration. Patrons draw a picture that matches the article's content. Completed projects are added to a DIY poster or bulletin board by library staff. Participants are invited to fill out "I Did a DIY Activity!" slips. Because instructions are included in activity sheets, no separate instruction sheet is necessary.

Materials Needed

- Activity sheets
- Crayons

A Few Days Ahead

- Photocopy activity sheets.

Opening Day

- Place activity sheets and crayons at the DIY station.

Tips and Flourishes

- Our activity sheet contains a simple fabricated news story. You could make up your own story, or use a real newspaper story (with permission from the publisher) or a story from the library newsletter.

- If time and resources allow, ask patrons to write their own news articles and illustrate them. These articles could reflect real events or imaginary happenings.

   A reproducible activity sheet is found on the following page; feel free to copy or adapt it.

Picture This!

Below is a news article . . . but no picture! Can you draw a picture to go with the story? When you're finished, put your project in the raffle box at the DIY station. Also fill out an "I Did a DIY Activity!" slip for your chance to win a prize!

Walking Broccoli Comes to the Library

Last Wednesday, a large stalk of broccoli stalked into the library. When the librarian asked the vegetable if it needed help, the broccoli responded that it just wanted to find a good book to read. When asked what type of book it was looking for, the broccoli simply said, "A green one."

After looking at several shelves of books, the broccoli selected a large green volume. The vegetable declined to comment on what the book was about.

After checking out the book, the broccoli walked to a nearby park and read.

It remains to be seen whether this piece of broccoli will return its book on time and whether it will check out more books in the future.

Activity 4: A Little Advice

Age Level: Elementary through Teen

Activity Time: 5–10 minutes

What It Is: This is a writing activity in which guests provide advice in the style of a newspaper advice column.

How It's Done: Participants pick up activity sheets and pencils at the DIY station. Each activity sheet contains three different "Dear Reader" queries. Library guests are invited to respond to any or all of the questions. Completed activity sheets and "I Did a DIY Activity!" slips are left in the raffle box. Staff posts activity sheets throughout the month.

Materials Needed

- Activity sheets
- Patron instructions
- Pencils
- Examples of advice columns from real newspapers, laminated or mounted on cardstock

A Few Days Ahead

- Generate patron instructions, or copy the ones included in this book.
- Cut out and laminate or mount child-appropriate advice columns from real newspapers.

Opening Day

- Display instructions and advice column examples at or near the DIY station.
- Place activity sheets in an easily accessed place on the table along with pencils.

As the Month Progresses

- Library staff collects completed activity sheets from the raffle box and posts them near the DIY station as part of a poster or bulletin board.

Tips and Flourishes

- Compile patrons' responses and bind them into a book for browsing or checkout. If space allows, include one or two responses in the library newsletter.
- This activity can be extended by having library visitors write questions for other patrons or librarians to answer on a bulletin board. For example, a patron might write, "Dear Reader, I just finished a great book about a vampire, and I'm looking for another vampire book to read. Do you have any suggestions?" Then, librarians and/or other patrons can answer the question by writing their suggestions below the query.

Reproducible patron instructions and an activity sheet are found on the following pages; feel free to copy or adapt them.

A Little Advice

Many newspapers have advice columns. People write to the newspaper asking for help or advice, and someone at the newspaper (an advice columnist) writes back with suggestions. At the DIY station, we have several advice columns from real newspapers on display.

Now it's your turn to be an advice columnist!

Take an activity sheet and a pencil from the DIY station. Read the questions and respond to one, two, or all three with your best advice! Use the library catalog to help you if you like.

When you are finished, put your activity sheet in the raffle box. Be sure to fill out an "I Did a DIY Activity!" slip and put that in the raffle box, too; you could win a fabulous prize!

A Little Advice

Dear Reader,

I love to read nonfiction books! I especially love books about animals. The last book I read was about bears. I loved it because it had a lot of details and great pictures. Can you suggest any books for me to read?

Thank you,

Nonfiction Ned

_____

_____

Dear Reader,

I would like to read a really great book. It doesn't matter if it is a long book, a short book, fiction, or nonfiction. Please tell me what your favorite book is!

Thank you,

Favorite Frederica

_____

_____

Dear Reader,

I am interested in finding a few new recipes in cookbooks. The problem is, I can't seem to find any cookbooks in the library! Can you help? Maybe if you could tell me the Dewey decimal number of the cookbooks, I could find them.

Thank you,

Recipe Reginald

_____

_____

I Did a DIY Activity!

If you did an activity at the DIY station, please fill out this form and drop it in the raffle box. You might win a fabulous prize!

My name is _____.

I am _____ years old.

My phone number is _____.

The activity I did was:
- ❐ The Classifieds
- ❐ Headliners
- ❐ Picture This!
- ❐ A Little Advice

I Did a DIY Activity!

If you did an activity at the DIY station, please fill out this form and drop it in the raffle box. You might win a fabulous prize!

My name is _____.

I am _____ years old.

My phone number is _____.

The activity I did was:
- ❐ The Classifieds
- ❐ Headliners
- ❐ Picture This!
- ❐ A Little Advice

I Did a DIY Activity!

If you did an activity at the DIY station, please fill out this form and drop it in the raffle box. You might win a fabulous prize!

My name is _____.

I am _____ years old.

My phone number is _____.

The activity I did was:
- ❐ The Classifieds
- ❐ Headliners
- ❐ Picture This!
- ❐ A Little Advice

I Did a DIY Activity!

If you did an activity at the DIY station, please fill out this form and drop it in the raffle box. You might win a fabulous prize!

My name is _____.

I am _____ years old.

My phone number is _____.

The activity I did was:
- ❐ The Classifieds
- ❐ Headliners
- ❐ Picture This!
- ❐ A Little Advice

From *DIY Programming and Book Displays: How to Stretch Your Programming without Stretching Your Budget and Staff* by Amanda Moss Struckmeyer and Svetha Hetzler. Santa Barbara, CA: Libraries Unlimited. Copyright © 2010.

Newspaper Book List

Are you looking for a great book about newspapers? Try these! If you need help finding them, use our online catalog or ask a reference librarian. Of course, we also have real newspapers at the library; they're a great place to find the latest news happening in the city, state, nation, and world!

Ada, Alma Flor. *Extra! Extra! Fairy-Tale News from Hidden Forest*. Atheneum, 2007. Primary.

Hidden Forest News has all the latest headlines and stories on mysterious bean sprouts and other local happenings.

Christensen, Bonnie. *The Daring Nellie Bly: America's Star Reporter*. Knopf, 2003. Primary/Upper Elementary.

A biography of Nellie Bly, a stunt reporter for the *New York Times* in the 1800s who traveled around the world faster than anyone had before.

Clements, Andrew. *The Landry News*. Simon & Schuster, 1999. Upper Elementary.

Burned-out teacher Mr. Larson gets a dose of reality and a much-needed nudge to improve his teaching practices, thanks to a newspaper editorial written by one of his students.

Giff, Patricia Reilly. *Eleven*. Wendy Lamb Books, 2008. Upper Elementary.

Sam discovers a mysterious newspaper clipping just before his 11th birthday, which leads him to find out some secrets about his family's past.

Kelly, John. *Scoop! An Exclusive by Monty Molenski*. Candlewick, 2007. Primary.

Reporter Monty Molenski is looking for a good story to write for the newspaper. Will he find one right under his nose?

Kraft, Erik. *Lenny and Mel: After-School Confidential*. Simon & Schuster, 2004. Primary.

Lenny and Mel need to find an after-school club to join, so they choose the newspaper club. The zany duo reports on happenings around the school in a ridiculously funny way.

Nelson, Blake. *The New Rules of High School*. Viking, 2003. Teen.

Max Caldwell is a 17-year-old model student: He's captain of the debate team, on the honor roll, and the incoming editor of the school paper. During his senior year, however, some things start to change in Max's approach to life.

Pratchett, Terry. *The Truth: A Novel of Discworld*. HarperCollins, 2000. Teen/Adult.

A satire set in a fantastical city full of zombies, werewolves, and vampires. The owner of the city's newspaper finds the printing press to be much faster than his old engraving technique. While this seems like a positive development at first, much drama unfolds over the changes at the paper.

Rooney, Andrew. *Pieces of My Mind*. Atheneum, 1984. Teen/Adult.

A collection of newspaper articles written by Andy Rooney.

Trelease, Jim, ed. *Read All About It! Great Read-Aloud Stories, Poems, and Newspaper Pieces for Preteens and Teens*. Penguin, 1993. Upper Elementary/Teen/Adult.

A unique collection of fiction, autobiography, and newspaper columns, perfect for reading aloud.

From *DIY Programming and Book Displays: How to Stretch Your Programming without Stretching Your Budget and Staff* by Amanda Moss Struckmeyer and Svetha Hetzler. Santa Barbara, CA: Libraries Unlimited. Copyright © 2010.

10

October: Monsters

Silly, scary, troubled, and misunderstood, literary monsters come in all shapes and sizes and, naturally, attract patrons of all ages because of their complexity. Monsters, beasts, and unusual creatures can be easily found in new and classic children's, teen, and adult literature.

October as Monster Month coincides with the Halloween season, but feel free to use this theme any time of the year. The activities and displays presented in this chapter will help highlight the library's selection of monster books.

A reproducible page of "I Did a DIY Activity!" slips and a booklist can be found at the end of this chapter.

DISPLAY IDEAS FOR MONSTER MONTH

Two of the activities this month involve finished products that will become part of the library's display. Activity 1 ("Welcome to the Monster Motel") serves as an interactive display as patrons contribute to the growing occupancy of the motel. Activity 4 ("Monster Munchies") is a creative and culinary activity. Participants create or find recipes that are fit for a monster and add them to the "Monster Munchies" recipe box at the DIY station. Patrons enjoy flipping through the recipe box and are inspired to come up with their own contribution.

In both of these activities, contributors leave their submission in a basket for staff to hang or file. Asking patrons to leave their finished activities for staff to post serves two purposes. It allows library staff to keep track of activity at the DIY station and ensures that submitted material is appropriate for display.

Activity 5 ("Guess How Many Cookies Are in Cookie Monster's Cookie Jar") attracts library visitors to your DIY station. Setting out a variety of cookie jars is an easy way to create an inviting display.

EXTENSIONS ON THE THEME

Consider using the results from Activities 2 and 3 ("Monster Books" and "Make Up a Monster Story") to enhance the library's newsletter and Web site. The answers from the "Monster Books" activity serve as a readers' advisory tool for patrons wishing to read peer-recommended books. The "Make Up a Monster Story" activity is a terrific way to feature the writing talent of your young contributors. You may also consider hosting a "fill-in-the-blank" program where participants play well-known games like Hangman and Mad Libs.

A monster story time is enjoyable for older preschoolers and elementary school-aged children. Many activities can be incorporated into this program, including silly snacks and short films. Many monster-themed and slightly scary story time films are available through Weston Woods and come with public performance rights. Movement activities give young patrons a chance to release some restlessness between books. Consider a "Monster Mash" dance-off for a book break. Snacks add a festive dimension to library programs. To round out the story time event, invite patrons to a "Beast Feast." Consider using the ideas submitted for the "Monster Munchies" DIY activity—just make sure recipes are edible for humans!

For teens, consider hosting a "Creature Feature." If the library has a movie license, consider showing new and old monster movies. For a "Retro-Monster Movie Night," you might show classics such as *King Kong, Godzilla,* or *Frankenstein.* Consider a "Then and Now" discussion after watching the films to compare the old and new versions of the same stories.

A "Book to Film" event also works well for 'tweens and teens; watch the film and invite patrons to discuss, contrast, and compare the books and films. Be prepared for fun and lively discussions.

Activity 1: Welcome to the Monster Motel

Age Level: Pre-K through Teen

Activity Time: 5–15 minutes

What It Is: This drawing activity encourages originality and creativity. It also helps build community, as each participant's contribution adds to the quantity and quality of the display.

How It's Done: Patrons pick up a construction paper "window" or "door" at the DIY station, along with crayons. The participant folds the paper along the top or side to create a window or door. Inside the windows and doors, patrons draw monsters that are occupying the "Monster Motel." Patrons may also decorate the outside of the windows and doors. Patrons leave their completed projects in a basket at the DIY station. Staff collects the completed activities and adds them to the wall or bulletin board near the DIY station. Patrons are invited to complete an "I Did a DIY Activity!" sheet and place them in the raffle box.

Materials Needed

- Poster board (36" × 24") for "Monster Motel"
- 9" × 12" construction paper, cut in half to 9" × 6"
- Crayons
- Glue stick or scotch tape for staff to hang windows and doors
- Patron instruction sheet
- Shallow basket for collecting finished projects

A Few Days Ahead

- Identify wall space near the DIY station for the "Monster Motel."
- Prepare poster board for the "Monster Motel"; windows and doors will be glued or taped to the poster board by library staff.
- Cut construction paper in half and fold a few sheets as examples.
- Generate instructions, or copy the instructions included in this book.

Opening Day

- Display instructions in a clear sign holder or on a wall near the DIY station.
- Place construction paper, crayons, and a basket for completed "Monster Motel" windows and doors at the DIY station.

As the Month Progresses

- Add completed activities to the growing display.

Because of the size and materials used for this activity, no reproducible patterns are included. A standard-size poster board may serve as the "Monster Motel," and the windows and doors may be constructed from standard-size 9" × 12" construction paper in assorted colors.

Tips and Flourishes

- Consider completing a window or door ahead of time to put on display. This will help patrons understand the activity.

Activity 1: Welcome to the Monster Motel (*Continued*)

- Display a variety of monster books for ideas and inspiration. A reproducible booklist is included at the end of this chapter.
- If time and resources allow, consider cutting the construction paper in various shapes and sizes for added interest. Having a basket of patterned paper, stickers, beads, buttons, and other embellishments adds dimension to the activity.

Booklist

Displaying monster guidebooks, monster poetry, and books on drawing monsters can help inspire creativity and participation. Browse through the art, poetry, fiction, and picture book collections, or try the titles listed here:

Ames, Lee. *Draw 50 Beasties and Yugglies and Turnover Uglies and Things That Go Bump in the Night.* Doubleday, 1988.

Ashman, Linda. *The Essential Worldwide Monster Guide.* Simon and Schuster Books for Young Readers, 2003.

Drake, Ernest. *Dr. Ernest Drake's Monsterology: The Complete Book of Monstrous Beasts, Illustrated.* Candlewick Press, 2008.

Emberley, Ed. *Ed Emberley's Drawing Book of Weirdos.* Little Brown, 2002.

Florian, Douglas. *Monster Motel: Poems and Paintings.* Harcourt Brace Jovanovich, 1993.

Gervais, Ricky. *Flanimals.* G. P. Putnam's Sons, 2005.

Lichtenheld, Tom. *Everything I Know about Monsters: A Collection of Made-Up Facts, Educated Guesses, and Silly Pictures about Creatures of Creepiness.* Simon and Schuster Books for Young Readers, 2003.

McCarty, Peter. *Jeremy Draws a Monster.* Henry Holt, 2009.

McNaughton, Colin. *Making Friends with Frankenstein: A Book of Monstrous Poems and Pictures.* Candlewick, 1994.

Olander, Johan. *A Field Guide to Monsters: Googly-Eyed Wart Floppers, Shadow-Casters, Toe-Eaters, and Other Creatures.* Marshall Cavendish, 2007.

Peffer, Jessica. *Dragonart Fantasy Characters: How to Draw Fantastic Beings and Incredible Creatures.* IMPACT, 2007.

Shane, V. *Fantastic Realms! Draw Fantasy Characters, Creatures, and Settings.* Impact Books, 2006.

Sierra, Judy. *Monster Goose.* Harcourt, 2001.

Thatch, James Otis. *A Child's Guide to Common Household Monsters.* Front Street, 2007.

Walker, Kevin. *Drawing and Painting Fantasy Beasts: Bring to Life the Creatures and Monsters of Other Realms.* Barron's, 2005.

Whitman, Candace. *Lines That Wiggle.* Blue Apple Books, 2009.

Patron instructions follow; feel free to copy or adapt them.

Welcome to the Monster Motel.
There's Always a Vacancy!

1. Choose a construction paper window or a door from the tray.

2. Fold your window or door along the top or side.

3. Use crayons to create a monster inside the window or door. You can also decorate the outside of the window or door.

4. Leave your completed window or door in the basket, and we'll add it to the Monster Motel.

5. Complete an "I Did a DIY Activity" sheet and place it in the raffle box for a chance to win a prize.

Activity 2: Monster Books

Age Level: Pre-K through Teen

Activity Time: 5 minutes

What It Is: In this literature-appreciation activity, library visitors have a chance to let library staff know what they enjoy reading, making this a great opportunity for role reversal.

How It's Done: Participants pick up "Monster Books" activity sheets and write down favorite monster books. Patrons are invited to complete an "I Did a DIY Activity!" sheet and place it in the raffle box. A book display will encourage participation.

Materials Needed

- Activity sheets
- Pencils

A Few Days Ahead

- Generate an activity sheet, or copy the one included in this book. Instructions for this activity are included in the activity sheet.
- Set up a display of monster books.

Opening Day

- Display instructions in a sign holder on the DIY table.
- Set out activity sheets and pencils at the DIY station.

Tips and Flourishes

- Compile patron responses into a bookmark or booklist. Peer-suggested titles are great readers' advisory tools.
- Extend the activity sheet question for older participants by asking what they specifically liked about the book and who or what age group they would recommend the book to.
- Consider posting photos of participants and their recommended book on your library's Web site. Remember to obtain signed permission forms to allow photos to be displayed.

A reproducible activity sheet follows; feel free to copy or adapt it.

Monster Books

Do you like to read books with monsters in them? Please tell us the title of one of your favorite monster books. Put your slip in the raffle box; we'll have a drawing at the end of October for a monstrous prize!

A monster book I like is _____.

My name: _____ My age: _____

My phone number: _____

Monster Books

Do you like to read books with monsters in them? Please tell us the title of one of your favorite monster books. Put your slip in the raffle box; we'll have a drawing at the end of October for a monstrous prize!

A monster book I like is _____.

My name: _____ My age: _____

My phone number: _____

Activity 3: Make Up a Monster Story

Age Level: Pre-K through Upper Elementary

Activity Time: 5–10 minutes

What It Is: This is a fill-in-the-blank writing activity similar to Mad Libs, a popular word game where substitution words are inserted to create a humorous story.

How It's Done: Patrons pick up activity sheets and pencils at the DIY station. The blank spaces are filled in to complete the story. Stories may be left in the basket at the DIY station for staff to display. Alternatively, participants may take their stories home. Contributors are invited to complete an "I Did a DIY Activity!" sheet and place it in the raffle box.

Materials Needed

- Patron activity sheets
- Pencils
- Basket for completed stories

A Few Days Ahead

- Generate an activity sheet, or copy the one included in this book. Instructions are included in the activity sheet.

Opening Day

- Set out activity sheets, pencils, and a basket at the DIY station.

Tips and Flourishes

- Ask patrons to illustrate their story. Consider providing colored pencils or crayons at the DIY station.
- Consider having patrons work with a partner so that the partner only asks for a part of speech or type of word (noun, adjective, verb) without reading the rest of the story. The results are always outrageous!
- Ask older patrons to continue the story or make up their own fill-in-the blank story.
- Publish completed stories in your library's newsletter.

A reproducible activity sheet follows; feel free to copy or adapt it.

Make Up a Monster Story

Using the categories listed below, fill in the blanks to complete the monster story. Make it as silly as you like!

A: Name a color

B: Any name

C: Noun

D: Noun

E: Noun

F: Name of a place

G: Silly expression

H: Plural noun

Once upon a time, there was a (A) _____ monster. The monster's name was (B) _____. It liked to eat (C) _____, (D) _____, and (E) _____. The monster's favorite place to go was (F) _____.

When the monster saw its friends, it always said, (G) "_____

_____."

The monster liked to read books about (H) _____.

The End

From *DIY Programming and Book Displays: How to Stretch Your Programming without Stretching Your Budget and Staff* by Amanda Moss Struckmeyer and Svetha Hetzler. Santa Barbara, CA: Libraries Unlimited. Copyright © 2010.

Activity 4: Monster Munchies

Age Level: Kindergarten through Teen

Activity Time: 5–15 minutes

What It Is: This culinary and creative activity encourages library visitors to share a favorite recipe. Even patrons who don't have cooking experience can participate by finding an interesting recipe from a book or creating something gruesome on their own.

How It's Done: Participants pick up recipe cards (index cards) and write recipes. Contributors leave their completed recipe cards at the DIY station, either in a basket or in a "Monster Munchies" recipe box. Library staff files the recipes randomly, alphabetically, or by category (i.e., appetizers, main dishes, lunches, breakfasts, and desserts). After completing the activity, participants fill out "I Did a DIY Activity!" sheets and place them in the DIY raffle box.

Materials Needed

- A small basket for blank recipe cards
- A file box for completed recipe cards
- Index cards or recipe cards
- Pencils and pens
- Patron instruction sheet

A Few Days Ahead

- Decorate the "Monster Munchies" recipe box.
- Generate patron instructions, or copy the instructions included in this chapter.

Opening Day

- Display instructions in a clear sign holder or on a wall near the DIY station.
- Place index cards, basket, pencils, pens, and "Monster Munchies" recipe box at the DIY station.

As the Month Progresses

- Add completed recipe cards to the "Monster Munchies" recipe box.

Because of the materials used for this activity, no reproducible patterns are included. Consider using lined 3" × 5" index cards for recipe entries. Use a small plastic file box to collect recipes.

Tips and Flourishes

- Consider completing a recipe or two for the recipe box. This will help patrons understand the activity and encourage participation.
- Stickers are an easy and inexpensive way to decorate the recipe box. Whimsical stickers are easily available at scrapbooking and hobby supply stores.
- Consider binding recipe submissions into a *Monster Munchies Cookbook* for your library's collection.
- Host a potluck "Beast Feast." Patrons can prepare and bring in their "Monster Munchies" recipe to share.

Activity 4: Monster Munchies (*Continued*)

Booklist

Displaying books about monsters and food will provide inspiration for your patrons and will encourage circulation. Browse through your library's picture book, fiction, and nonfiction cookery collection, or try the titles listed here:

Bowers, Sharon. *Ghoulish Goodies.* Storey, 2009.

Dahl, Roald. *Revolting Recipes.* Viking, 1994.

Hicks, Barbara Jean. *Jitterbug Jam.* Farrar, Straus and Giroux, 2005.

Hicks, Barbara Jean. *Monsters Don't Eat Broccoli.* Alfred A. Knopf, 2009.

Monroe, Lucy. *Creepy Cuisine.* Random House, 1993.

Rex, Adam. *Frankenstein Makes a Sandwich: And Other Stories You're Sure to Like, Because They're All about Monsters and Some of Them Are Also about Food.* Harcourt, 2006.

Rex, Adam. *Frankenstein Takes the Cake.* Harcourt, 2008.

Sierra, Judy. *Thelonius Monster's Sky-High Fly Pie: A Revolting Rhyme.* Knopf, 2006.

Villicich-Solomon, Tina. *Creepy Cookies.* Random House, 1996.

Zalben, Jane Breskin. *Saturday Night at the Beastro.* Harper Collins, 2004.

Patron instructions follow; feel free to copy or adapt them.

Monster Munchies . . . Recipes to Satisfy a Monster's Appetite!

1. Take a blank recipe card from the basket.

2. Write down a recipe of your own or one you found.

3. Be sure to include ingredients and instructions.

4. Feel free to give your recipe a name.

5. Place your completed recipe in the "Monster Munchies" recipe box.

6. Fill out an "I Did a DIY Activity!" sheet and drop it in the raffle box for your chance to win a prize.

Activity 5: Guess How Many Cookies Are in the Monster's Cookie Jar

Age Level: Pre-K through Teen

Activity Time: 5 minutes

What It Is: This is an estimation activity encouraging patrons of all ages to guess the number of cookies in a jar.

How It's Done: Patrons pick up guessing slips and pencils from the DIY station. After taking a good look at the cookie jar, patrons write down their estimations on the guessing slips and are invited to place their guesses in the raffle box for a chance to win the cookies in the cookie jar.

Materials Needed

- Quart-size mason jar or airtight plastic container
- One box of cookies (plain cookies like Vanilla Wafers work well)
- Guessing slips
- Pencils

A Few Days Ahead

- Generate guessing slips, or photocopy the ones included in this book.
- Fill the cookie jar, being sure to count and record the number of cookies in the jar.

Opening Day

- Display cookie jar, guessing slips, and pencils at the DIY station.

Tips and Flourishes

- Consider filling jars with cookies in assorted sizes for more of a challenge.
- Consider displaying multiple jars with different types of cookies for added interest. The variety may attract more patrons to the DIY station.
- Consider filling a jar with chocolate chips to make the estimation activity more challenging for older patrons.
- Consider hosting a monster cookie-decorating program by supplying plain round sugar cookies, different-colored frosting, candy eyeballs, sprinkles, gummy worms, and jelly beans. These supplies can be found in specialty baking and confectionary supply stores.

Booklist

Displaying books about cookies will tie in with your guessing jar activity. There are many picture books and fiction titles about cookies. Be sure to also include some cookbooks. Here is a list of suggested titles:

Amendt, Linda J. *400 Sensational Cookies*. Robert Rose, 2009.

Bloom, Carole. *Bite-Size Desserts: Creating Mini Sweet Treats, from Cupcakes and Cobblers to Custards and Cookies*. Wiley, 2009.

Dadey, Debbie. *The Bride of Frankenstein Doesn't Bake Cookies*. Scholastic, 2000.

Activity 5: Guess How Many Cookies Are in the Monster's Cookie Jar (*Continued*)

Dionne, Erin. *Models Don't Eat Chocolate Cookies.* Dial Books for Young Readers, 2009.

Dunbar, Fiona. *The Truth Cookie.* Orchard, 2005.

Dunnington, Rose. *The Greatest Cookies Ever: Dozens of Delicious, Chewy, Chunky, Fun and Foolproof Recipes.* Lark Books, 2005.

Ferber, Brenda. *Julia's Kitchen.* Farrar Straus Giroux, 2006.

Goodman, Susan. *All in Just One Cookie.* Greenwillow Books, 2005.

Lewis, Sarah. *Kids Baking: 60 Delicious Recipes for Children to Make.* Hamllyn, 2006.

Palatini, Margie. *Bad Boy Gets Cookie!* Katherine Tegen Books, 2006.

Rosenthal, Amy Krouse. *Cookies: Bite-Size Life Lessons.* Harper Collins, 2006.

Wellington, Monica. *Mr. Cookie Baker.* Dutton Children's Books, 1992.

White, Lois. *The Ultimate Cookie Book.* Meredith Books, 2007.

Williamson, Sarah. *Bake the Best-Ever Cookies!* Williamson, 2001.

Patron instructions and reproducible activity sheets follow; feel free to copy or adapt them.

How Many Cookies Are in the Jar?

Your name: _____

Your age: _____ Your phone number: _____

Number of cookies you think are in the jar: _____

How Many Cookies Are in the Jar?

Your name: _____

Your age: _____ Your phone number: _____

Number of cookies you think are in the jar: _____

How Many Cookies Are in the Jar?

Your name: _____

Your age: _____ Your phone number: _____

Number of cookies you think are in the jar: _____

How Many Cookies Are in the Jar?

Your name: _____

Your age: _____ Your phone number: _____

Number of cookies you think are in the jar: _____

I Did a DIY Activity!

If you did an activity at the DIY station, please fill out this form and drop it in the ballot box. You might win a monstrously fabulous prize!

My name is _____.

I am _____ years old. My phone number is _____.

Draw a circle around the activities you did:

Welcome to the Monster Motel

Monster Books

Make Up a Monster Story

Monster Munchies

Guess How Many Cookies Are in the Monster's Cookie Jar

I Did a DIY Activity!

If you did an activity at the DIY station, please fill out this form and drop it in the ballot box. You might win a monstrously fabulous prize!

My name is _____.

I am _____ years old. My phone number is _____.

Draw a circle around the activities you did:

Welcome to the Monster Motel

Monster Books

Make Up a Monster Story

Monster Munchies

Guess How Many Cookies Are in the Monster's Cookie Jar

Monstrously Good Reads!

Asma, Stephen T. *On Monsters: An Unnatural History of Our Worst Fears.* Oxford University Press, 2009. Adult.

A detailed history of monsters, spanning from 326 B.C. to modern times.

Davis, Eleanor. *Stinky: A Toon Book.* Raw Junior, 2008. Upper Elementary.

In this graphic novel, Stinky the monster comes up with a crazy plan to scare away the human kid that enters his smelly swamp.

Funke, Cornelia Caroline. *Ghosthunters* Series. Scholastic, 2007. Upper Elementary.

Shy and clumsy Tim learns the trade of ghost hunting and is soon called on to dispel monsters from his house and from his town.

Loery, Dean. *Nightmare Academy* Series. Harper Collins, 2007. Upper Elementary.

Charlie is sent to the Nightmare Academy where he learns to harness his powers to return monsters to the Netherworld.

Numberman, Neil. *Do Not Build a Frankenstein.* Greenwillow Books, 2009. Primary.

A boy warns his neighbors of the hazards that come with building your own monster.

Rex, Adam. *Goodnight Goon: A Petrifying Parody.* G. P. Putnam's Sons, 2008. Primary.

In this parody of Margaret Wise Brown's *Goodnight Moon,* the young monster says goodnight to all the "monster-ish" items in his room.

Sendak, Maurice. *Where the Wild Things Are.* Harper & Row, 1963. Primary.

Maurice Sendak's classic story about Max who finds himself on an island inhabited by monsters and soon becomes "King of the Wild Things."

Soo, Kean. *Jellaby.* Hyperion Books for Children, 2008. Upper Elementary.

Shy Portia moves to a new town and soon befriends a purple monster named Jellaby in this graphic novel.

Taylor, Greg. *Killer Pizza.* Feiwel and Friends, 2009. Teen.

Toby's summer job at Killer Pizza, a local pizza restaurant, turns out to be a front for a monster-hunting organization.

Willems, Mo. Your Pal Mo Willems Presents Leonardo the Terrible Monster. Hyperion, 2005. Primary.

Leonardo is a terrible monster. . . . He can't even scare a nervous little boy!

Young, Judy. *The Hidden Bestiary of Marvelous, Mysterious, and (Maybe Even) Magical Creatures.* Sleeping Bear Press, 2009.

Using clues from Basil Bernard Barnswhitten's journal, readers accompany and help track down all the mysterious creatures on his list.

11

November: Libraries

November is a time to express gratitude. As advocates of the library, this is the perfect opportunity for library visitors to show thankfulness and appreciation for the bounty of materials and resources the public library has to offer and share with its community. The DIY activities this month include creating a top-10 list, a "Thanksgiving Bounty" of books, a fill-in-the-blank story, and a word game using the letters from the word *library*. A reproducible booklist of library-themed books can be found at the end of this chapter.

DISPLAY IDEAS FOR LIBRARY MONTH

Activity 1 is "Top-10 List: Why I Am Thankful for the Library" and can serve as a display. Once patrons have had a chance to contribute, compile the results to display. The result will be similar to top-10 lists from late-night talk shows. Consider using black poster board that resembles a chalkboard to write down patrons' responses. You may need to expand your display to a top-20 or more list if the activity attracts many visitors. Participants are always happy to see their responses on display.

Activity 2, "Thanksgiving Bounty of Books," is also an interactive display. If you have a long display table, you can put a seasonal tablecloth and decorations to depict the harvest, and patrons can display the books they are thankful for. For added seasonal whimsy, fill a large cornucopia or basket with books to portray the library's bounty. Alternately or additionally, participants may draw a picture representing their book and their artwork can be hung near the book display.

Many companies that provide furnishing and decoration items for libraries also sell decorative display products that showcase and highlight the uniqueness of public libraries. If resources allow, consider purchasing items from such companies as Demco, Upstart, Highsmith, or ALA to help encourage inspiration and participation.

EXTENSIONS ON THE THEME

Many programs can easily fit this month's DIY theme. Offering a library-themed story time for young children is a fun and easy way share the appreciation staff and patrons feel toward the library. For 'tweens and teens, a library party with a book or CD swap is fun. Invite local teen bands to perform at the party to round out the event.

A "Thanksgiving Feast" of books and food is a great community-building event. Invite families, children, and adults to a potluck dinner and showcase books from Activity 2, "A Thanksgiving Bounty of Books." Your potluck event will quickly turn into a great opportunity for participants to booktalk their favorite books.

You may also consider a "Library Luncheon." The luncheon could consist of a library tour that may include behind-the-scenes viewings of office spaces, technical services, book drops, and staff lounge areas. Kids especially get a kick out of the book drop and staff lounge! After the tour, invite your guests to have lunch with library staff. Organize the luncheon to match the library's budget. An informal brown bag–style luncheon where attendees bring their own lunch and the library provides drinks and dessert is an inexpensive way to host the event. If resources allow, a formal, catered luncheon may be an attractive choice. For a formal luncheon, use place cards that resemble library cards and thematic tables representing various library departments and activities. Encourage and invite the entire library staff to mingle with guests. The event is a great opportunity to show library users how much the library staff appreciates their patronage.

Activity 1: Top-10 List: Why I Am Thankful for the Library

Age Level: Pre-K through Teen

Activity Time: 5 minutes

What It Is: This is a library-appreciation activity that may also be used as a display. The result is a list of reasons why patrons are thankful for the library. The #1 reason is the most popular reason, #2 the second most popular, and so on.

How It's Done: Patrons pick up a "Top-10 List" contribution slip and write down why they are thankful for the library. Participants are invited to drop their slip in the raffle box for a chance to win a prize. After the activity is complete, library staff compiles the answers and displays the top-10 list. The list can be placed near the DIY station.

Materials Needed

- Patron instructions
- "Top-10 List" contribution slip
- Pencils
- Poster board for staff use
- Crayons or markers for staff use

A Few Days Ahead

- Generate patron instructions, or copy the instructions included in this book.
- Generate "Top-10 List" contribution slips, or copy the slips included in this book.

Opening Day

- Display instructions, contribution slips, pencils, and raffle box near the DIY station.

Tips and Flourishes

- Consider keeping a daily running tally of the responses received if there is a lot of DIY activity. This will help when it's time to create the "Top-10 List" poster.
- For an old-fashioned blackboard look, use black poster board and white crayon.
- If there is a lot of activity, consider expanding the list beyond 10 items. All participants will appreciate seeing their response on display.
- Consider asking staff to participate with a similar activity, "Top-10 List: Why I Am Thankful for Library Patrons," and post the responses side by side.
- Host a "Top-10 Reasons Why I'm Thankful for My Library" T-shirt-designing program using the responses from the DIY activity. Provide fabric markers and ask participants to bring in white shirts to design their shirts.

Patron instructions and reproducible activity sheets follow; feel free to copy or adapt them.

Top-10 List: Why I Am Thankful for the Library

1. Think of why you use the library.

2. Pick up a "Top-10 List" contribution slip and write down why you are most thankful for the library.

3. After filling out the slip, place it in the raffle box for your chance to win a prize.

4. Next time you visit the library, be sure check out the "Top-10 List" at the DIY station and see where your response ranks.

Top-10 List: Why I Am Thankful for the Library

The reason I am thankful for the library is:

_____

Your name: _____

Your age: _____ Your phone number: _____

Top-10 List: Why I Am Thankful for the Library

The reason I am thankful for the library is:

_____

Your name: _____

Your age: _____ Your phone number: _____

Top-10 List: Why I Am Thankful for the Library

The reason I am thankful for the library is:

_____

Your name: _____

Your age: _____ Your phone number: _____

Activity 2: A Thanksgiving Bounty of Books

Age Level: Pre-K through Teen

Activity Time: 5–15 minutes

What It Is: This is a literature-appreciation activity that encourages patrons to share favorite authors and titles with others in their library community. It also helps build community, as each participant's contribution adds to the quantity and quality of the display.

How It's Done: Patrons find one of their favorite books in the library and place it in a basket on the "Thanksgiving Table." If patrons cannot find one of their favorites, they can simply write down the name of the book and the author on a "Favorite Book and Author" slip and library staff may find it at a later time. Patrons are invited to place their completed "Favorite Book and Author" slips in the raffle box for a chance to win a prize.

Materials Needed

- Seasonal basket to hold favorite books
- "Favorite Book and Author" slips
- Pencils
- Patron instruction sheet
- Seasonal tablecloth and table decorations for the display

A Few Days Ahead

- Identify space near the DIY station for the "Thanksgiving Table."
- Generate instructions, or copy the instructions included in this book.
- Generate "Favorite Book and Author" slips, or copy the ones included in this book.

Opening Day

- Display instructions in a clear sign holder or on a wall near the DIY station.
- Place "Favorite Book and Author" slips, pencils, and the raffle box at the DIY station.
- Decorate your "Thanksgiving Table" and have at least one basket out. You may wish to put one of your favorite books in the basket to help patrons understand the activity.

Tips and Flourishes

- Create bookmarks with the titles and authors supplied by patrons.
- Create a booklist for your library's Web site. Peer-recommended titles make great readers' advisory tools.
- Host a "Read-a-thon." Bring in the bountiful basket of books for the program and offer seasonal snacks for your readers.
- Consider contacting a local bakery for a prize donation. A slice of pie or maybe even a whole pie is a fun and seasonal participation prize that ties in with the idea of the Thanksgiving bounty.

Patron instructions and reproducible activity sheets follow; feel free to copy or adapt them.

A Thanksgiving Bounty of Books

1. Think of a favorite title and author.

2. Try and find the book in the library stacks, or ask your librarian to help you find it.

3. Place your book in the basket and fill out a "Favorite Book and Author" slip.

4. If all of your favorite books are currently checked out, you can still fill out a "Favorite Book and Author" slip. Your librarian will add the book to the bountiful book basket when it is returned.

5. Place your "Favorite Book and Author" slip in the raffle box for your chance to win a prize.

A Thanksgiving Bounty of Books: My Favorite Book and Author

My favorite book is _____.

My favorite author is _____.

My name is _____.

My age is _____. My phone number is _____.

A Thanksgiving Bounty of Books: My Favorite Book and Author

My favorite book is _____.

My favorite author is _____.

My name is _____.

My age is _____. My phone number is _____.

A Thanksgiving Bounty of Books: My Favorite Book and Author

My favorite book is _____.

My favorite author is _____.

My name is _____.

My age is _____. My phone number is _____.

Activity 3: A Trip to the Library:
A Fill-in-the-Blank Story

Age Level: Pre-K through Upper Elementary

Activity Time: 10–15 minutes

What It Is: This is a writing activity that asks patrons to fill in the blank spaces to create a story.

How It's Done: Patrons pick up a "A Trip to the Library: A Fill-in-the-Blank Story" sheet and fill in the blanks using the word choices provided. This activity can be done alone or with a partner. The story can be left in the basket at the DIY station for staff to hang. Alternatively, participants may take them home. Patrons are invited to fill out the information at the bottom of the story sheet and place it in the raffle box for a chance to win a prize.

Materials Needed

- Patron instructions
- "A Trip to the Library: A Fill-in-the-Blank Story" sheets
- Pencils
- A shallow basket to collect completed stories

A Few Days Ahead

- Make copies of "A Trip to the Library: A Fill-in-the Blank Story."
- Generate instruction sheets, or make copies of the ones included in this book.

Opening Day

- Display instructions in a clear sign holder or on a wall near the DIY station.
- Place story sheets, pencils, and raffle box at the DIY station.
- Place a shallow basket to collect the completed stories at the DIY station.

Tips and Flourishes

- Host a "Fill-in-the-Blank Story" program. Invite participants back to the library so contributors can hear all the fill-in-the-blank stories.

   Patron instructions and reproducible activity sheets follow; feel free to copy or adapt them.

A Trip to the Library: A Fill-in-the-Blank Story

Instructions

1. Choose one name or word from each category to complete your story. Once you choose a name or word for a specific letter, that will be the name or word you use for that letter throughout the story.

2. For example, if you choose "Sally" for A, (A) will be Sally for the entire story.

3. Work with a partner if you like.

4. If you prefer, circle your choices before reading the story. Then, transfer your circled word choices to the story and read it.

5. Fill out your information at the end of the activity sheet. Tear off at the dotted line, and place the slip in the raffle box for your chance to win a prize.

6. You can take your story home, or you may leave it in the raffle box. We will display your story for others to read.

A Trip to the Library: A Fill-in-the-Blank Story

Word Choices

A: your name, your friend's name, your sibling's name, your cousin's name

B: exploded, disappeared, cracked, melted

C: cleaning the oven, folding laundry, scrubbing the toilet

D: organizing the tool shed, cleaning out the garage, spackling the walls

E: ball, bone, rope, Frisbee

F: take a nap, chew on a shoe, howl, chase his (or her) tail

G: solitaire, dominoes, jacks, piano

H: cleaned his or her bedroom, fed the fish, picked up the dog poop in the backyard

I: name of a neighbor

J: comic books, magazines

K: excited, adventurous, like a superstar

L: snakes, cooking, cars, history

M: name of one of your favorite authors

N: magazines, DVDs

O: graphic novels, Nintendo games

P: your librarian's name

Q: bucket, crate, shopping cart, wheelbarrow

R: funktastic, cool, awesome

* If "A" is a boy, use the pronouns *he* and *his* to complete the story. If "A" is a girl, use the pronouns *she* and *her* to complete the story.

From *DIY Programming and Book Displays: How to Stretch Your Programming without Stretching Your Budget and Staff* by Amanda Moss Struckmeyer and Svetha Hetzler. Santa Barbara, CA: Libraries Unlimited. Copyright © 2010.

A Trip to the Library:
A Fill-in the Blank Story

(A) _____'s Trip to the Library: A Fill-in-the-
Blank Story

It was the Saturday after Thanksgiving, and (A) _____ was

bored. [His/Her] cousins drove back home earlier that day, and the TV had just

(B) _____. (A) _____'s mom was tired of seeing

(A) _____ moping around, so she suggested

(C) _____. "No thanks," mumbled (A) _____.

Dad was pretty busy fixing things around the house but thought

(D) _____ might help cure (A) _____'s boredom.

"Maybe some other time," said (A) _____. Rover,

(A) _____'s dog, brought over his (E) _____. "Not

right now Rover," said (A) _____. Rover sighed and curled

back up on the couch. He couldn't understand why (A) _____

couldn't just (F) _____ like he did when he was bored.

(A) _____ played some (G) _____, which

was okay for a while. (A) _____ even

(H) _____. Of course, there were other chores to do, but

(A) _____ was looking for excitement.

A few minutes later, (A) _____ looked out the window

and saw (I) _____, [his/her] neighbor.

From *DIY Programming and Book Displays: How to Stretch Your Programming without Stretching Your Budget and Staff* by Amanda Moss Struckmeyer and Svetha Hetzler. Santa Barbara, CA: Libraries Unlimited. Copyright © 2010.

A Trip to the Library: A Fill-in the Blank Story (*Continued*)

(I) _____ looked super happy and was carrying a heavy bag.

(A) _____ ran outside. "Hey, what's in your bag?" asked

(A) _____. "A bunch of

(J) _____. I can't wait to go home and look at all of

them."

"That's it!" thought (A) _____. "I'm going to go to the library." Just walking into the library made (A) _____ feel

(K) _____. [He/She] went in and began searching the shelves.

He/she found nonfiction books about (L) _____.

(A) _____ picked up some books by (M)

_____, [his/her] favorite author. [He/She] also

picked out some (N) _____ and

(O) _____. By the time (A) _____

was ready to check out, he/she could barely walk or see over [his/her] stack of

books,

(N) _____, and (O) _____. Luckily, (P)

_____ had a

(Q) _____ to offer (A) _____.

A Trip to the Library: A Fill-in the Blank Story (*Continued*)

This Thanksgiving weekend, (A) _____ knew [he/she] was

thankful for [his/her] library and all the (R) _____ things

he/she could check out. Of course, it sure beat

(C) _____!

The End

Fill out, cut, and place the portion below in the raffle box for your chance to win a prize.

Your name: _____

The title of your story: _____

Your age: _____ Your phone number: _____

From *DIY Programming and Book Displays: How to Stretch Your Programming without Stretching Your Budget and Staff* by Amanda Moss Struckmeyer and Svetha Hetzler. Santa Barbara, CA: Libraries Unlimited. Copyright © 2010.

Activity 4: How Many Words Can You Make Using the Letters from the Word *LIBRARY?*

Age Level: Elementary through Teen

Activity Time: Varies

What It Is: This is a word game activity encouraging patrons of all ages to come up with as many words as possible using the letters in the word *library*.

How It's Done: Patrons pick up an activity sheet and a pencil from the DIY station and write down words using the letters L, I, B, R, A, R, and Y in any combination. Patrons are invited to place their completed activity sheets in the raffle box for a chance to win a prize.

Materials Needed

- Activity sheets (instructions for this activity are included in the activity sheet)
- Pencils

A Few Days Ahead

- Generate activity sheets, or photocopy the ones included in this book.

Opening Day

- Display activity sheets and pencils at the DIY station.

Tips and Flourishes

- Consider using other library-related words like *reference, story time, circulation, catalog,* etc.

A reproducible activity sheet follows; feel free to copy or adapt it.

How Many Words Can You Make Using the Letters from the Word *LIBRARY*?

Instructions

1. Think of words two letters long or longer using only the letters L-I-B-R-A-R-Y.

2. You may only use the number of letters used in the word *library*. For example, you can only use one *L, I, B, A,* or *Y*. You may use two *R*s since there are two Rs in *LIBRARY*.

3. As you think of words, write them down in the spaces provided. Feel free to write on the back or add additional sheets if necessary.

4. When you have thought of as many words as you can, fill out the information at the bottom of the sheet, fold the sheet, and place it in the raffle box for your chance to win a prize.

Words Using L-I-B-R-A-R-Y

_____

_____

_____

_____

_____

_____

_____

Your name: _____

Your age: _____ Your phone number: _____

Books Celebrating Libraries and Librarians

Child, Lauren. *But Excuse Me, That Is My Book.* Dial Books for Young Readers, 2006. Primary.

The popular sibling duo, Charlie and Lola, are excited to visit the library, but problems arise when Lola's favorite book is not on the shelf.

Gonzalez, Lucia M. *The Storyteller's Candle/La velita de los cuentos.* Children's Book Press, 2008. Primary.

A bilingual historical-fiction picture book based on the true story of Pura Belpre. During the Great Depression, Pura Belpre introduces the public library to immigrants living in the neighborhood and hosts the neighborhood's first Three Kings' Day fiesta.

Graber, Janet. *Muktar and the Camels.* Henry Holt, 2009. Primary.

When a traveling librarian arrives with books and an injured camel at an orphanage in Kenya, 11-year-old Muktar helps the injured camel and proves himself.

Gutman, Dan. *Mrs. Roopy Is Loopy.* Harper Trophy, 2004. Upper Elementary.

Mrs. Roopy sure seems loopy. She is always pretending to be a famous person, and A.J. and his classmates are convinced she is crazy.

Knudsen, Michelle. *Library Lion.* Candlewick Press, 2006. Primary.

When a friendly lion starts visiting the local library, the librarian isn't sure what to do.

Krosoczka, Jarrett. *Lunch Lady and the League of Librarians.* Alfred A. Knopf, 2009. Upper Elementary.

The school lunch lady is also a secret crime fighter, and she's on the case to solve suspicious library activity.

Lewis, J. Patrick. *Please Bury Me in the Library.* Harcourt, 2005. Upper Elementary.

A collection of poems about libraries and books.

Myron, Vicki. *Dewey: The Small-Town Library Cat Who Touched the World.* Grand Central, 2008. Adult.

A memoir and tribute to Dewey, the library cat. When a kitten is deposited in the book drop, the Spencer Public Library and its patrons provide plenty of love and care.

Paratore, Coleen. *The Cupid Chronicles.* Simon & Schuster Books for Young Readers, 2006. Teen.

Thirteen-year-old Willa works hard to hold fund-raising events to keep her local library from closing.

Peck Richard. *Here Lies the Librarian.* Dial Books, 2006. Upper Elementary.

A nostalgic look at American life, set in 1914. Fourteen-year-old tomboy Eleanor discovers new possibilities after four librarians arrive in her small Indiana town.

12

December: Pets

A pet holds a special place in the family. Books and films about pets are timeless and attract patrons of all ages. Stories about pets evoke strong emotions, and often readers are laughing out loud or shedding quiet tears.

There are many local and national pet celebrations throughout the year, so feel free to use the DIY activities presented in this chapter any time of the year. The activities and displays presented in this chapter will help highlight your library's selection of pet books. A reproducible page of "I Did a DIY Activity!" slips and a booklist can be found at the end of the chapter.

DISPLAY IDEAS FOR PET MONTH

This month's first activity ("Pet Collage") results in finished products that become part of the library's interactive display. The pet photo and drawing submissions contribute to the growing collage, and the visible growth encourages participation. Library visitors love seeing their beloved pets honored at the library. Activity 4 ("Guess How Many Dog Biscuits Are in the Treat Jar") makes an inviting display for pet lovers. Dog owners have fun attempting to win treats for their canine companions.

EXTENSIONS ON THE THEME

The popularity of pets lends itself well to fun-filled programming. For children who want to practice reading and love dogs, set up a "Paws to Read" or "Reading with Rover" program. Most communities offer the services of therapy dogs to libraries. Interested participants sign up for 15-minute time slots and read to a therapy dog.

A pet-themed story time is a natural extension of this month's DIY. There are plenty of dog and cat picture books, which are great for sharing. Of course, when you think of pets, cats and dogs are obvious, but don't forget to include unusual and rare pets such as snakes, hamsters, pigs, and even crocodiles!

Try a "Play Literacy Goes to the Vet" program. This interactive program gives library visitors a chance to act or play out literature. For example, you can read *Bark George* by Jules Feiffer and set out toy medical kits, bandages, stuffed animals, clipboards, and pencils. You can also set up chairs to resemble a waiting area. Invite participants to bring in a favorite stuffed animal from home. Then sit back and enjoy watching the children act out the experience of taking their pet to the veterinarian.

Host an intergenerational book discussion program. Popular adult books are often adapted as children's books. *Marley and Me: Life and Love with the World's Worst Dog* by John Grogan and *Dewey: The Small-Town Library Cat That Touched the World* by Vicki Myron are recent examples.

Everyone loves showing off their pets, and hosting a "Pet Parade" is a fun way to extend the "Pet Collage" activity. For this event, you may need to obtain special permission from your town or city and have participants sign a participation form to eliminate possible liability issues. Having treats for the pets after the event adds a nice touch.

Activity 1: Pet Collage

Age Level: Pre-K through Teen

Activity Time: 5–15 minutes

What It Is: This art activity encourages creative collage, photography, or drawing while building community, as each participant's contribution adds to the quantity and quality of the display.

How It's Done: Patrons bring a photo of their pet to the library to submit for the "Pet Collage." Participants can write their pet's name on a label and attach the label to the photo. Alternatively, patrons may draw a portrait of their pet or their dream pet. This alternative allows patrons who don't have a pet to contribute. Patrons leave their completed projects in a basket at the DIY station. Staff collects the completed activities and adds them to the wall or bulletin board near the DIY station. Patrons are invited to complete an "I Did a DIY Activity!" sheet. Completed "I Did a DIY Activity!" sheets are placed in the raffle box for a chance to win a prize.

Materials Needed

- Labels for pets' names
- Pencils or pens to write down pets' names
- Paper, colored pencils, and crayons for pet drawings
- Patron instruction sheet
- Shallow basket for collecting finished projects

A Few Days Ahead

- Identify wall space near the DIY station for the "Pet Collage."
- Hang some pet photos or a pet poster as an example.
- Generate instructions, or copy the instructions included in this book.

Opening Day

- Display instructions in a clear sign holder or on a wall near the DIY station.
- Place paper, crayons, pencils, pens, labels, a basket for submissions, and raffle box at the DIY station.

As the Month Progresses

- Add completed activities to the growing collage.

Tips and Flourishes

- Ask library staff to submit photos of their pets to add the display. This helps library visitors understand the activity and also gives staff the opportunity to take part in a fun library event.
- Display a variety of pet books for ideas and inspiration. A reproducible booklist is included at the end of this chapter.
- Consider adding objects like collars, aquarium accessories, animal printed paper, and small pet toys to the collage for a 3-D effect.

- Prizes for participation can be pet toys and accessories featured in the "Pet Collage."
- To keep your activity as labor-free for library staff, let patrons know that photos will not be returned. Alternatively, if you would like to return the photos, plan a special day or event for contributors to visit the library to retrieve photos.

Patron instructions follow; feel free to copy or adapt them.

Pet Collage

Help us create a fun and furry collage with your favorite animal pals.

1. Submit a photo of your pet or pets. If you don't have a pet at your house, you can still participate by submitting a photo of a friend's, neighbor's, or relative's pet. If you prefer, you can draw a picture of your pet or perhaps even your dream pet! Use the paper, pencils, and crayons for your drawing.

2. Place a label with your pet's name on the picture, and place the photo or drawing in the basket. We'll add it to the Pet Collage for you.

3. Look for your pet in the collage the next time you visit the library.

4. Fill out an "I Did a DIY Activity" slip, and place it in the raffle box for your chance to win a pet-themed prize.

 * Please note, the photos and drawings will become part of the library's display and will not be returned.

From *DIY Programming and Book Displays: How to Stretch Your Programming without Stretching Your Budget and Staff* by Amanda Moss Struckmeyer and Svetha Hetzler. Santa Barbara, CA: Libraries Unlimited. Copyright © 2010.

Activity 2: Pets and Pages

Age Level: Pre-K through Teen

Activity Time: 5 minutes

What It Is: This is a matching activity. Patrons have a chance to show off their literary knowledge and their library searching skills by matching literary pets to the books that feature them.

How It's Done: Participants pick up a "Pets and Pages" activity sheet and match the pet with their book. Patrons are invited to complete an "I Did a DIY Activity!" sheet and place it in the raffle box.

Materials Needed

- Activity sheets
- Pencils

A Few Days Ahead

- Generate an activity sheet, or copy the one included in this book. Instructions for this activity are included in the activity sheet. There is one activity sheet for picture books and one for chapter books.

Opening Day

- Set out activity sheets and pencils at the DIY station.

Tips and Flourishes

- Consider a matching game featuring pets on film and television.
- Display the books featured on the activity sheets.
  Reproducible activity sheets follow; feel free to copy or adapt them.

Answer Key for "Picture Books and Pets"

Loveable Lyle by Bernard Waber: **Crocodile**

Ginger by Charlotte Voake: **Cat**

Biscuit Finds a Friend by Alyssa Capucilli: **Dog**

Julius by Angela Johnson: **Pig**

Charlie Hits It Big by Deborah Blumenthal: **Guinea Pig**

Answer Key for "Pets and Pages" Matching Game

Alpha Dog by Jennifer Ziegler: **Seamus**

Because of Winn-Dixie by Kate DiCamillo: **Opal**

Charlotte's Web by E. B. White: **Wilbur**

Four Ugly Cats in Apartment 3D by Marilyn Sachs: **Lily**

Harry Potter and the Sorcerer's Stone by J. K. Rowling: **Fang**

Henry Huggins by Beverly Cleary: **Ribsy**

Activity 2: Pets and Pages (*Continued*)

I, Jack by Patricia Finney: **Stopes Family**

Lady Lollipop by Dick King Smith: **Penelope**

Pippi Longstocking by Astrid Lingren: **Mr. Nilsson**

The Tales of Olga da Polga by Michael Bond: **Karen Sawdust**

The World According to Humphrey by Betty Birney: **Mrs. Brisbane**

Picture Books and Pets

Do you know what types of pets are characters in each of these books? If you don't, here's a hint: The featured pets are a cat, crocodile, dog, guinea pig, and pig. Draw a picture of the correct animal below each title. Fill out an "I Did a DIY Activity" sheet, and place it in the raffle box for your chance to win a prize.

Loveable Lyle by Bernard Waber

Ginger by Charlotte Voake

Biscuit Finds a Friend by Alyssa Capucilli

Julius by Angela Johnson

Charlie Hits It Big by Deborah Blumenthal

Pets and Pages Matching Game

Match the pets (or their humans) to their books.

Place your completed sheet in the basket, then fill out an "I Did a DIY Activity" sheet and place it in the ballot box for your chance to win a pet-themed prize.

(Column A)	(Column B)
Alpha Dog by Jennifer Ziegler	Fang
Because of Winn-Dixie by Kate DiCamillo	Karen Sawdust
Charlotte's Web by E. B. White	Lily
Four Ugly Cats in Apartment 3D by Marilyn Sachs	Mr. Nilsson
Harry Potter and the Sorcerer's Stone by J. K. Rowling	Mrs. Brisbane
Henry Huggins by Beverly Cleary	Opal
I, Jack by Patricia Finney	Penelope
Lady Lollipop by Dick King Smith	Ribsy
Pippi Longstocking by Astrid Lingren	Seamus
The Tales of Olga da Polga by Michael Bond	Stopes Family
The World according to Humphrey by Betty Birney	Wilbur

Activity 3: Create Your Dream Pet

Age Level: Pre-K through Teen

Activity Time: Varies

What It Is: A questionnaire and creative drawing activity in which library guests think of the qualities they find most desirable in a pet and then draw their real or imaginary pet.

How It's Done: Patrons pick up an activity sheet and pencil at the DIY station. Participants answer a few questions to determine their ideal pet's physical characteristics and personality traits. Once they've answered the questionnaire, patrons are invited to draw and name their dream pet. Activity sheets may be left in the basket at the DIY station for staff to display. Contributors are invited to complete an "I Did a DIY Activity!" sheet and place it in the raffle box.

Materials Needed

- Patron activity sheets
- Pencils
- Crayons or colored pencils
- Basket for completed activity sheets

A Few Days Ahead

- Generate an activity sheet, or copy the one included in this book. Instructions are included in the activity sheet.

Opening Day

- Set out activity sheets, pencils, and crayons at the DIY station.

Tips and Flourishes

- Ask patrons to come up with additional characteristics about their pet.
- Provide small pieces of cardstock so participants may turn their dream pet into trading cards with a picture on the front and their features on the back.
- Host a trading card–swapping program.

A reproducible activity sheet follows; feel free to copy or adapt them.

My Dream Pet

Answer the following questions to help you determine your ideal pet. Then draw your pet according to the answers from the questionnaire. Give your pet's breed a name and your pet a name. Leave your activity sheet in the basket so we can hang it up. Fill out an "I Did a DIY Activity" sheet, and place it in the raffle box for your chance to win a prize!

My pet _____ the water. (loves or hates)

My pet is _____. (furry or smooth)

My pet loves to _____. (sleep or run)

My pet loves _____ weather. (hot or cold)

My pet loves to eat _____. (your choice of food)

My pet has a great sense of _____. (hearing, vision, taste, smell, or touch)

My pet loves a _____. (party or a quiet night at home)

Draw your dream pet according to your answers. For example, if you answered "My pet loves the water," you can give your pet some fins or gills.

Your pet's name: _____

Breed of your pet: _____

Activity 4: Guess How Many Dog Treats Are in the Treat Jar

Age Level: Pre-K through Teen

Activity Time: 5 minutes

What It Is: This is an estimation activity encouraging patrons of all ages to guess the number of dog treats in a jar.

How It's Done: Patrons pick up a guessing slip and pencil from the DIY station. After taking a good look at the treat jar, participants write down their estimations on the guessing slip and are invited to place their guesses in the raffle box for a chance to win the treats in the treat jar.

Materials Needed

- A quart-size glass mason jar or airtight plastic container
- One box of medium or small dog biscuits
- Guessing slips
- Pencils

A Few Days Ahead

- Generate or photocopy guessing slips.
- Fill the treat jar, being sure to count and record the number of treats in the jar.

Opening Day

- Display treat jar, guessing slips, and pencils at the DIY station.

Tips and Flourishes

- Consider filling jars with treats in assorted sizes.
- Consider displaying multiple jars with different types of treats for added interest. You may also choose to add treats for different types of pets; the variety may attract more patrons to the DIY station.

Patron instructions and reproducible activity sheets follow; feel free to copy or adapt them.

How Many Dog Treats Are in the Jar?

Your name: _____

Your age: _____ Your phone number: _____

Number of treats you think are in the jar: _____

How Many Dog Treats Are in the Jar?

Your name: _____

Your age: _____ Your phone number: _____

Number of treats you think are in the jar: _____

How Many Dog Treats Are in the Jar?

Your name: _____

Your age: _____ Your phone number: _____

Number of treats you think are in the jar: _____

How Many Dog Treats Are in the Jar?

Your name: _____

Your age: _____ Your phone number: _____

Number of treats you think are in the jar: _____

I Did a DIY Activity!

Your name: _____

Your age: _____ Your phone number: _____

Place a checkmark next to the DIY activity you completed, and place this slip in the jar for a chance to win a fabulous prize for your pet!

Pet Collage: _____ Pets and Pages: Picture Books _____

Create Your "Dream Pet": _____ Pets and Pages: Matching Game _____

Guess the Number of Dog Treats in the Jar: _____

I Did a DIY Activity!

Your name: _____

Your age: _____ Your phone number: _____

Place a checkmark next to the DIY activity you completed, and place this slip in the jar for a chance to win a fabulous prize for your pet!

Pet Collage: _____ Pets and Pages: Picture Books _____

Create Your "Dream Pet": _____ Pets and Pages: Matching Game _____

Guess the Number of Dog Treats in the Jar: _____

Books about Pets for Animal Lovers

Birney, Betty. *The World according to Humphrey.* G. P. Putnam's Sons, 2004. Upper Elementary.

Humphrey, a classroom hamster, has many adventures with the students and teachers of Longfellow School.

Bourke, Anthony. *Christian the Lion.* Henry Holt, 2009. Upper Elementary.

A true story that recounts the unexpected and unusual relationship between two humans and a lion cub.

DiCamillo, Kate. *Because of Winn Dixie.* Candlewick, 2000. Upper Elementary.

Ten-year-old India moves to Naomi, Florida, and describes all the good things that start happening to her after she finds a homeless dog she names Winn-Dixie.

Feiffer, Jules. *Bark George.* Harper Collins, 1999. Primary.

George's mother and the vet are surprised when they find out why George doesn't bark.

Flesher, Vivienne. *Alfred's Nose.* Katherine Tegen Books, 2008. Primary.

Alfred, a French bulldog, is unhappy with his unusual looks, especially his nose.

Grogan, John. *Marley and Me: Life and Love with the World's Worst Dog.* Morrow, 2005. Adult.

A heartwarming story of a family's life with their mischievous yellow lab named Marley.

Harper, Charise Mericle. *Fashion Kitty.* Hyperion Paperbacks for Children, 2005. Upper Elementary.

Kiki, the superhero fashion kitty, saves other cats and kittens from fashion disaster in this graphic novel.

Henkes, Kevin. *Kitten's First Full Moon.* Greenwillow Books, 2004. Primary.

After mistaking the full moon for a bowl of milk, an unlucky and hungry kitten finally gets lucky.

Sidman, Joyce. *The World According to Dog: Poems and Teen Voices.* Houghton Mifflin, 2003. Teen.

A collection of poems and essays written by teens about the dogs in their lives.

Stevens, Janet. *Help Me Mr. Mutt! Expert Answers for Dogs with People Problems.* Harcourt, 2008. Primary.

An advice column written by and for dogs. Mr. Mutt helps his fellow canines with their human problems.

Author and Title Index

Subject Index

About the Authors

 AMANDA MOSS STRUCKMEYER is a youth services librarian at Middleton Public Library, Wisconsin. In 1999 she graduated from the College of Saint Benedict in Saint Joseph, Minnesota, with a bachelor of arts in elementary education; she received her masters of library science from the University of Wisconsin–Madison in 2005. In addition, she served on the 2009 Newbery Award Committee and was on the first-ever World Championship–winning book cart drill team from UW–Madison.

 SVETHA HETZLER is head of youth services, Middleton Public Library, Wisconsin. She received a bachelor of science in anatomy and physiology from Boston University and a masters degree in library and information science degree from the University of South Florida. She recently completed a two-year term on the Charlotte Zolotow Awards Committee.